Nonfiction

Dressing Up: Transvestism and Drag: The History of
  an Obsession
London: The Biography
Albion: The Origins of the English Imagination
Thames: The Biography

Biography

Ezra Pound and His World
T. S. Eliot
Dickens
Blake
The Life of Thomas More
Shakespeare: The Biography

Poetry

Ouch!
The Diversions of Purley and Other Poems

Criticism

Notes for a New Culture
The Collection: Journalism, Reviews, Essays, Short Stories,
  Lectures (edited by Thomas Wright)

NAN A. TALESE

DOUBLEDAY

New York   London   Toronto   Sydney   Auckland

Peter Ackroyd

Poe

A Life Cut Short

Published in the United States by Nan A. Talese,
an imprint of The Doubleday Publishing Group,
a division of Random House, Inc., New York.
www.nanatalese.com

Originally published in Great Britain by Chatto & Windus, London,
in 2008.

DOUBLEDAY is a registered trademark of Random House, Inc.

Book design by Maria Carella

Library of Congress Cataloging-in-Publication Data
Ackroyd, Peter, 1949–
   Poe : a life cut short / Peter Ackroyd. — 1st ed.
       p.   cm.
Includes index.
1. Poe, Edgar Allan, 1809–1849. 2. Authors, American—19th century—
Biography. I. Title.
PS2631.A65 2008b
818'.309—dc22
[B]   2008018244

ISBN 978-0-385-50800-1

PRINTED IN THE UNITED STATES OF AMERICA

10 9 8 7 6 5 4 3 2 1

First Edition in the United States of America

CONTENTS

Poe

CHAPTER ONE

The Victim

On the evening of 26 September 1849, Edgar Allan Poe stopped in the office of a physician in Richmond, Virginia—John Carter—and obtained a palliative for the fever that had beset him. Then he went across the road and had supper in a local inn. He took with him, by mistake, Dr. Carter's malacca sword cane.

Poe was about to embark on the steamboat to Baltimore. This was the first stop on his way to New York, where he had business to transact. The boat was to leave at four o'clock on the following morning, for a journey that would last approximately twenty-five hours. He seemed to the friends who saw him off to be cheerful and sober. He expected to be away from Richmond for no more than two weeks. Yet he forgot to take his luggage with him. This was the last verifiable sighting of Poe until he was found dying in a tavern six days later.

. . .

He arrived in Baltimore on Friday, 28 September. He lingered in this city, instead of making his way to Philadelphia, the next stop on his way to New York, and there are accounts of his drinking. He may have been drinking to ward off the effects of the fever. He may have feared a precipitate heart attack. He had been told, by the doctors in Richmond, that his next seizure would prove fatal.

It is possible that he then travelled by train to Philadelphia. He visited some friends in that city, and became drunk or ill. On the following morning, in his bewildered state, he declared that he was going on to New York. But in fact, by accident or design, he returned to Baltimore. There are unsubstantiated reports that he then tried to return once more to Philadelphia but was found "insensible" on the train. The conductor took him back to Baltimore. The truth is lost. Everything is in a mist.

Neilson Poe, his cousin, later wrote to Poe's mother-in-law and unofficial guardian, Maria Clemm, that "at what time he arrived in the city [Baltimore], where he spent the time he was here, or under what circumstances, I have been unable to ascertain." Despite much research and speculation, no further light has been thrown upon the matter. He may have been wandering through the streets, or making his unsteady way from tavern to tavern. All that is known for certain is that, on 3 October, a newspaper printer sent a message to Joseph Evans Snodgrass: "There is a gentleman, rather the worse for wear, at Ryan's 4th ward polls, who goes under the cognomen of Edgar A. Poe, and who appears to be in great distress, & he says he is acquainted with you, and I assure you, he is in need of immediate assistance." Snodgrass had been the editor of the *Saturday Visiter*, to which Poe had contributed. "Ryan's 4th ward polls" refers to a tavern that was being used as a polling place for Congressional elections taking place that day; Ryan was the name of the proprietor of the tavern.

The printer's note was sufficiently serious to summon Snodgrass. He entered the barroom and found Poe sitting, stupefied, with a crowd of "drinking men" around him. His odd clothes caught Snodgrass's attention. He was wearing a tattered straw hat, and a pair of badly fitting trousers. He had a secondhand coat, but no sign of waistcoat or neckcloth. With the possible exception of the straw hat, these were not the clothes with which he had left Richmond. Yet, surprisingly, he still held Dr. Carter's malacca cane. In his inebriated and beleaguered state, it might have seemed to him an instrument of defence.

Snodgrass did not approach him, but ordered a room for him in the same tavern. He was about to send word to Poe's relatives in Baltimore, when two of them coincidentally arrived. One was Poe's cousin Henry Herring, who had come to the tavern on electoral business. He was related to a local politician. Snodgrass recalled that "they declined to take private care of him" on the grounds that he had in the past been abusive in this state of intoxication; instead they advised that Poe be removed to a local hospital. They managed to get him into a carriage, carrying him "as if a corpse," and he was admitted to Washington College Hospital.

The resident physician, John Moran, later reported that Poe remained "unconscious of his condition" until early the following morning. His stupor was then succeeded by "tremor of the limbs" as well as delirium with "constant talking—and vacant converse with spectral and imaginary objects on the walls." Only on the second day after his admission, Friday, 5 October, did he recover his tranquillity. He began to talk, but he was not coherent. He told the doctor that he had a wife in Richmond, which was not true, and that he did not know when he had left that city. The doctor then reassured him that he would soon be in the company of friends, at which point he broke out in an agony of self-reproach at his degradation, protesting that the best thing a friend might do for him was to blow out his (Poe's) brains. Then he fell into a slumber.

On waking he passed into delirium. On the Saturday evening he began to call out "Reynolds," and did so continually until three on the following Sunday morning. "Having become enfeebled from exertion," the doctor wrote, "he became quiet and seemed to rest for a short time, then gently moving his head he said *'Lord Help my poor Soul'* and expired." This is the testimony of Dr. Moran, written to Maria Clemm five weeks after the events he related. Despite later embellishments by the doctor it is the closest approximation to the truth now available.

. . .

What had Poe been doing for the lost days in Baltimore? The most commonly accepted theory is that he was used as a "stooge" for polling purposes, being dressed up in someone else's clothes so that he might vote more than once for a particular candidate. These false voters were held in "coops" or inns, where they were nursed with alcohol. It also transpired that "Reynolds," the name Poe continued to repeat in his final delirium, was the surname of one of the voting officials at Ryan's tavern.

It is a possible explanation but not the only one. It has been suggested, for example, that he had a large amount of money from subscriptions to the *Stylus,* a magazine that he was preparing, and that as a consequence he was robbed. There are also many explanations for an early death, including delirium tremens and tuberculosis, "lesion of the brain" or a brain tumour, and diabetes. The well is too deep for the truth to be recovered.

A funeral was held on Monday, 8 October, with only four mourners. Among these were Henry Herring and Neilson Poe. The ceremony lasted for no more than three or four minutes. Like his narratives and fables, Poe's own story ends abruptly and inconclusively; it is bedevilled by a mystery that has never been, and probably can never be, resolved.

CHAPTER TWO

The Orphan

Edgar Allan Poe has become the image of the *poète maudit*, the blasted soul, the wanderer. His fate was heavy, his life all but insupportable. A rain of blows descended on him from the time of his birth. He once said that "to revolutionise, at one effort, the universal world of human thought" it was necessary only "to write and publish a very little book. Its title should be simple—a few plain words—'My Heart Laid Bare.' But—this little book must be *true to its title*." Poe never wrote such a book, but his life deserved one.

His torment—a mixture of insatiable anxiety and no less helpless longing—began early. His mother had already contracted tuberculosis before his birth, and it may be surmised there was some loss or lack of nourishment in the womb. The perils of a confined space, in which a victim lies panting, play a large part in his fictions. Both his parents, David and Eliza Poe, were also labouring under a heavy weight of anxiety exacerbated by poverty. Circumambient tension affects the unborn child. So the haunted life of Poe began before his birth. "I do believe God gave me a spark of genius," he said a few weeks before his death, "but He quenched it in misery."

He was born on a cold day, 19 January 1809, in a lodging house in Boston. A storm had filled Boston Harbor with icedrifts. In later reports Poe changed the year of his birth, almost at whim, as if he did not wish to look at the event too closely. His parents were both actors, travelling players whose status was just a little higher than that of vagabonds. He may have been named after Mr. Edgar, the manager of the theatrical troupe with which the Poes were associated. Certain of his contemporaries noticed that, in later life, Poe manifested a theatrical or histrionic air. "The world shall be my theatre," he once wrote. "I must either conquer or die."

There is an old theatrical adage that the show must go on. Three weeks after Poe's birth a Boston newspaper wrote that "we congratulate the frequenters of the theatre on the recovery of Mrs. Poe from her recent confinement." She was playing the part of Rosalinda in a play entitled *Abaellino the Great Bandit*. But the wandering life of the Poes had an immediate effect upon their infant son, since soon after his birth he was dispatched to the care of his paternal grandparents in Baltimore, Maryland, for some months. It was the first of many rejections suffered by Poe. Yet, perhaps in consequence, he venerated his mother. He once wrote in a newspaper article that he was "the son of an actress, had invariably made it his boast, and no earl was ever prouder of his earldom than he of his descent from a woman who, although well born, hesitated not to consecrate to the drama her brief career of genius and of beauty." He was putting the best possible interpretation upon his mother's behaviour.

. . .

Of course Eliza Poe was not well born at all. She had sailed in 1796 from England to America in the company of her mother, an actress of Covent Garden, in the hope or expectation that there would be greater opportunities for the dramatic arts in the new country. She was only nine at the time of her migration, but she soon became a practised artiste. Within three months of her arrival in the United States, she was performing on stage. There is one extant portrait of her in her early maturity. It shows a pretty if slight young woman, with fashionable ringlets; she has a lively expression, only slightly spoiled by somewhat protuberant eyes. She wears an Empire-line robe and a pert little bonnet. She must have been a competent and pleasing actress, since she gained many plaudits in the newspapers of the time. She was also versatile, sometimes sustaining three roles in the same evening. In the course of her relatively short career she assumed some 201 different parts. One of her fellow players was Mr. Luke Usher, whose name has since come down to posterity.

In 1802, at the age of fifteen, she married a fellow actor, Charles Hopkins, who died three years later. On 14

March 1806, six months after the death of her first husband, the young actress married David Poe in Richmond, Virginia, in what seem to have been hasty circumstances. David Poe had to borrow money for the occasion. He was intended for a legal career, but was diverted from it by theatrical ambitions. They were only partly fulfilled, however, and the newspaper reports suggest that he was no match for his pretty young wife. One magazine decided that he "was never destined for the high walks of drama." He was twenty-two at the time of the marriage, three years older than his wife. But he was already an impetuous and extravagant young man, much given to drinking. Performances were cancelled at short notice because of what the manager called Mr. Poe's "sudden indisposition," a euphemism for total intoxication. It is a matter of debate whether the propensity for heavy drinking, or for alcoholism (which is not the same thing), can be inherited. The only extant letter in David Poe's hand is a desperate plea for money, with the assurance that "nothing but extreme distress would have forc'd me to make this application." It is precisely the kind of letter his son was obliged to write in later years. It might be said that Poe became an echo of his father, as eerie a connection as any in his own fictions.

Henry, the first child of David and Eliza Poe, was born in January 1807. Two years after his birth he was consigned to the care of David Poe's parents, Elizabeth and "General" Poe. The wandering life of the theatrical Poes, travelling up and down the East Coast from New York to Boston, from Baltimore to Philadelphia and Richmond, and back again, had proved too tiring for mother and infant alike.

"General" Poe was not a general at all but a former maker of spinning wheels; at the time of the United States War of Independence he was appointed as Deputy Quartermaster General for the city of Baltimore, and was later promoted to the rank of major. Yet he was an enterprising and successful officer, later earning the commendations of the Marquis de Lafayette. He must also have been successful in the no less challenging role of parent, since in all but name he adopted Henry and he cared for Edgar in the earliest months of his life.

In the summer of 1809 David and Eliza returned to Baltimore for little Edgar. But it was not a happy family reunion. Husband and wife were both tubercular, their condition made infinitely worse by poverty and uncertain livelihood. In December 1810, another child was born, Rosalie, or "Rosie" as she was known, and stretched the resources of the young family still further. There are reports that the two youngest children were placed in the care of an old Welsh woman who "freely administered to them gin and other spirituous liquors, with sometimes laudanum" to render them "strong and healthy." Or, perhaps, simply to keep them quiet.

Then, at some point in the spring or early summer of 1811, David Poe disappeared. He never came back to his wife and family. The *Norfolk Herald* of 26 July reported that Mrs. Poe was "left alone . . . friendless and unprotected."

In later life, according to a colleague, Edgar Poe "pretended" not to know what had become of his father. There may not have been any pretence involved. The reasons for David Poe's flight are unknown. There were rumours of a quarrel with Eliza, and persistent gossip that Rosalie was not his child. It has even been suggested that he abandoned his family as early as 1810, perhaps before the birth of Rosalie.

Eliza was at the same time slipping into the final stages of her tubercular illness. The infant Edgar must have been acutely aware of the loss of his father and of the fading of his mother. He may not have been able to understand these things, but in these earliest years he was enveloped in an air of menace and fatality. Anxiety was his childhood bedfellow. He would have seen, too, the gradual wasting of her form with the painful spasmodic coughs and the effusion of blood. These images never left him. He resurrects the consumptive form of the beloved female in many of his tales.

Throughout July and October 1811, Eliza Poe still appeared on the stage at a theatre in Richmond. Then, in November, she retreated to her bed for ever. At the beginning of the month it was reported by one citizen of Richmond that she was "sick" and "destitute." By the end of November the *Richmond Enquirer* announced that "*Mrs. Poe*, lingering on the bed of disease and surrounded by her children, asks for your *assistance*; and *asks it perhaps for the last time*." Nine days later she was dead. The two small children were held up for a last view of the waxen corpse of their mother. Rosalie was given an empty jewel box, one of Mrs. Poe's few remaining possessions, and Edgar was given a miniature of his mother together with two locks of his parent's hair sealed in a pocketbook. On the back of the miniature she had painted a view of Boston Harbor, with the admonition to her infant son to "love Boston, the place of his birth." He never did obey that injunction. She was carried to St. John's churchyard, with her son and daughter in attendance.

In a letter written some twenty-four years later, Poe said of his mother, "I myself never knew her—and never knew the affection of a father. Both died . . . within a few weeks of each other. I have many occasional dealings with Adversity, but the want of parental affection has been the heaviest of my trials." It seems unlikely that the father died so soon after the mother. Poe was keen upon theatrical effect, even concerning those matters closest to him. But the other claim may be genuine. It is possible, even plausible, that he did not remember knowing his mother. Overwhelming grief may lead to the blessing of amnesia. Those early years may have remained quite obscure to him.

But they were understood by him in another sense. He hardly knew what the death of his mother meant at the time but, as the years passed, the sense of grief and of loss grew larger and more oppressive. There was something missing. Something precious had gone. He was a perpetual orphan in the world. All the evidence of his career, and of his writing, suggests that he was bound by ropes of fire to the first experiences of abandonment and of loneliness.

The image of the dead or dying woman, young and beautiful and good, fills his fictions. We may recall here the lines of Exeter in *King Henry V*:

And all my mother came into mine eyes,
And gave me up to tears.

And what of these unfortunate children, deserted first by a father and then unwillingly abandoned by a mother? In her last days, lying upon a straw mattress in a rented room, Eliza Poe had been visited and comforted by what were known in the newspapers as "ladies of the most respectable families." Among these was the wife of a merchant and businessman, John Allan, who had migrated from Scotland to the land of financial promise. Frances, or "Fanny," Allan had formed an attachment to the young Poe. She was then twenty-five years old but had no children of her own, and the sight of the forlorn infant had awakened strong sensations within her. She persuaded her husband that little Edgar should be given a home, while Rosalie was taken into the care of another Scottish mercantile family, the Mackenzies. So Edgar, then a small child, was removed to a house of strangers on the corner of Thirteenth Street and Main Street, above the business premises of Ellis and Allan. At his christening on 7 January 1812 he was given the name of his surrogate parents: he became Edgar Allan Poe.

. . .

The descriptions of the young boy, during these early years in the Allan household, are uniformly favourable. Neighbours in Richmond recalled him as "a lovely little fellow, with dark curls and brilliant eyes, dressed like a young prince"; he was characterised by charm and cleverness, blessed with an affectionate and generous temperament, noted for a frank and vivacious disposition. It sounds almost too good to be true. Little Lord Fauntleroy was nothing compared to him. He danced on the table, to the delight of Fanny Allan's female companions, and recited *The Lay of the Last Minstrel.* He toasted "the ladies" with a glass of sweet wine and water. He was petted, and dressed up, by Mrs. Allan. He seems also to have gained the affection of her husband. John Allan was thirty-one when Edgar joined the family. He was a man of business, but neither dour nor hard; on the contrary he seems to have been keen to the delights and pleasures of life. He already had two illegitimate children, living in Richmond. He must also have had some fellow feeling with the young Poe, since he himself was an orphan.

Other figures in the Allan family remain anonymous and elusive: they comprise the household of slaves who lived in partitioned quarters. Among them was the "mammy" deputed to care for the young Poe whenever Fanny Allan was elsewhere. We know that in the household lived a young slave called Scipio, and an older slave called Thomas. There were no doubt others. Poe always defended the institution of slavery, for which he seems to have harboured affectionate memories. He owed a larger debt, too, to the small black community in which his imagination was awakened by stories of graves and charnel houses.

Poe's maternal grandmother, Eliza Poe, described him as "the Child of fortune" in being fostered by such a kindly couple. But there is of course no record of *his* feelings on the matter. He must have been aware, however, that he was living on the charity and kindness of those who had no true relationship to him; this instilled in him a sense of uncertainty, or of defensiveness. It made him fearful. There is a childhood story of his being driven past a log cabin surrounded by graves, at the sight of which he screamed out, "They will run after us and drag me down!"

CHAPTER THREE

The Schoolboy

In the late spring of 1815 John Allan decided to remove himself and his family to England. There had been a slump in the fortunes of his business in Richmond, and the mercantile climate of London seemed more propitious. He wanted, in particular, to renew trading relationships with the tobacco importers of the capital. So at the end of June the Allans set sail on the *Lothair* for Liverpool, a journey that would take almost five weeks. The party consisted of John Allan, Frances Allan, Anne Moore Valentine in her capacity as sister and companion of Frances, and the black slave known only as Thomas. They took their small charge with them.

Poe was on the ocean for the first time. On the pilot boat, riding out to sea, John Allan reported that "Ned [Edgar] cared but little about it, poor fellow." But the sight of the waves and of the rolling horizon impressed itself upon the imagination of the boy who was to return to it in his future writing. When they arrived on the other shore Allan reported the six-year-old as asking "Pa say something for me: say I was not afraid coming across the Sea." This suggests that he was trying to conceal his fear.

They docked in Liverpool on 29 July, but did not travel directly to London. Instead John Allan decided to visit his relations in Scotland; there were sisters at Irvine and Kilmarnock, and other relatives in Greenock, from where they travelled on to Glasgow and Edinburgh. The Scottish grand tour lasted for some two months, and at the beginning of October the Allans took a carriage to London. They rented lodgings in Southampton Row, just south of Russell Square, where they all soon caught cold from the damp and heavy London air. There is a picture of the household, given by John Allan in a letter, where he describes "Edgar reading a little Story Book." It may be the book that Poe mentioned in an essay some years later, when he remarked on "how fondly do we recur in memory to those enchanted days of our boyhood when we first learned to grow serious over Robinson Crusoe!"

There was, however, more exacting reading. In early April 1816, Poe was enrolled at a boarding school in Sloane Street superintended by two sisters known as the "Misses Dubourg." An extant bill from this establishment includes such items as a "Separate Bed," a "Seat in Church," "Mavor's Spelling" and "Fresnoy's Geography." The rest of the curriculum is unknown, but Poe prospered under its regimen. In June 1818, John Allan told a correspondent that "Edgar is a fine Boy and reads Latin pretty sharply."

His progress was such that, a month later, "Edgar Allan" was enrolled for tuition in another school. He became a pupil of the Manor House School, in Stoke Newington, under the aegis of the Reverend John Bransby. It was located in what was then a country village, with an ancient church and a number of fine old houses; Daniel Defoe had once lived in the same street as the school. Here Poe studied Latin, among other orthodox subjects, and took dancing lessons. At a later date Bransby recalled his erstwhile pupil as "a quick and clever boy and would have been a very good boy if he had not been spoilt by his parents; but they spoilt him, and allowed him an extravagant amount of pocket money, which enabled him to get into all manner of mischief . . ." On another occasion he described the boy as "intelligent, wayward and wilful." These were all characteristics that would also be applied to Poe in later life. It was no doubt Fanny, rather than John, who pampered the child; the pocket money may have been "extravagant," however, by English rather than American standards.

Poe left his own account of the school, in heightened form, in "William Wilson," where he describes it as a ponderous and roomy establishment with innumerable floors and chambers and "no end to its windings." Poe was always acutely sensitive to buildings, and this "quaint" and "Gothic" structure gave him cause for much imaginative contemplation. He recalled the "dusky atmosphere" of this "misty-looking village," too, so Stoke Newington helped to inspire his first reveries. They were not, however, necessarily pleasant ones. He told a friend, in later years, that his school days in England had been "sad, lonely and unhappy."

His unhappiness was fully shared by Frances Allan. She was never able to reconcile herself to life in London, and as a consequence suffered from a number of unspecified ailments in the five years of residence. John Allan described "Frances complaining as usual" and, at later date, "complaining a good deal"; a female relative wrote that she is "very Weak—and is afraid she will feel much too fatigued to write." She went down to Cheltenham to sample the waters, but nothing could alleviate her distress. Her husband was of more sanguine temperament. In the autumn of 1818 John Allan reported that "Edgar is growing wonderfully and enjoys a reputation as both able and willing to receive instruction." A year later he remarks that Poe "is a very fine Boy and a good scholar."

His optimism did not perhaps extend to his own affairs, since in 1819 a sudden collapse in the price of tobacco on the London market threatened his business with ruin. His debts grew ever larger, and he determined to give up the mercantile life in order to become a farmer or planter. He prepared to leave England, and to return with his family to his adopted country. So, on 16 June 1820, they set sail from Liverpool on the *Martha*. They docked in New York almost six weeks later, and then took the steamboat to Richmond.

. . .

In this period Richmond was a slow-moving, sleepy, sultry place with a population of 10,000. It was in large part an industrial city, but half of its population were slaves. The American South was then a land of servitude, with all the torpor and casual violence associated with that condition. The city was built on eight green hills overlooking the James River, the houses clustered on the sides of the hills; the river was a consolation in what was often an oppressive climate, making its way past small islands and over broken boulders. The landscape at the height of summer, when the Poes returned, was decorated with the peach tree and the magnolia. There were many fine and well-built houses along the main streets of the town, with large gardens filled with roses and linden trees, myrtle and honeysuckle. There was a legislature, and a splendid public library; there were assembly rooms and white wooden churches. But, close to them, were the crumbling tenements and sheds where some of the black population lived.

The streets were filled with goats, and pigs, and horses. There were still cows grazing in Capitol Square as late as the middle of the nineteenth century. There were stage coaches, and carriages, with their black footmen and coachmen. The larger plantation houses were very spacious, with cool verandahs and rooms shielded from the glare of the sun by linen blinds. The men sat in rocking chairs, smoked their cigars and chewed on the local crop of tobacco. Elsewhere there were cabins for the slaves, where black children sprawled and played in the dust. There would always be a sense of settled dejection in such a place, lifted only by the constant supply of sherry cobblers and mint juleps. Drying tobacco poisoned the air.

The Allan family stayed at first in the house of John Allan's partner, Charles Ellis, and perhaps at his urging and instigation it was determined that Allan would remain at his mercantile post in order to steer the business to success. At the beginning of the autumn Poe was sent to a local school, Richmond Academy, where his master remembered him as "ambitious to excel, and although not conspicuously studious, he always acquitted himself well in his classes. He was remarkable for self-respect, without haughtiness"; he also described him as of "a very excitable temperament" with "a great deal of self-esteem." So he was sometimes a difficult and wilful child.

From this age, too, he was writing poetry. His schoolteacher described him as "born poet" who wrote verses "*con amore* and not as mere tasks." John Allan shared the master's high opinion, and showed him a manuscript of young Poe's poems with a view to eventual publication. This was deemed inadvisable, since it might lead to excessive flattery for an already over-excitable young boy. Allan's enquiry, however, emphasises the fact that he took his young charge's literary ambitions very seriously. He was not the authoritarian and distant figure of some biographers' invention.

At school Poe studied the standard classical authors, among them Ovid and Virgil and Cicero. But he also excelled in less scholastic pursuits. He was a good swimmer, and once swam six miles against the tide of the James River watched by masters and pupils alike. He was athletic, wiry and strong; he boxed, and excelled in field sports such as running. This is in marked contrast to the debility and almost continual ill health of his adult years. He was reported to be of "a very sweet disposition . . . always cheerful, brimful of mirth and a very great favourite with his schoolmates." He won prizes for elocution, and excelled at the declamation of the Latin poets and the Elizabethan dramatists.

But, as is invariably the case in the accounts of anyone's life, there were conflicting reports. One fellow pupil described him as "self-willed, capricious, inclined to be imperious, and though of generous impulses, not steadily kind, or even amiable." So the young Poe harboured a grudge against the world. His schoolfellows had learned, by some means or other, that he was the orphaned child of travelling players and that he had been "adopted" by the Allan family. For this reason the other boys "declined his leadership." The rejection encouraged a "fierceness" in him, taking the form of pride, or hauteur, but also rendered him sensitive and vulnerable to every slight. These were also the characteristics of the older Poe. Another contemporary recalled that the young Poe was "retiring in disposition and singularly unsociable in manner." It was remarked, in particular, that he never took any of his friends to his home after school. When he left the school grounds, his departure marked "the end of his sociability" for that day.

The schoolboy Poe went on long and sometimes solitary "tramps" through the woods above Richmond; with his friends he organised raids on the local orchards and turnip patches; he planned "fish-fries" by the banks of the James River. One schoolfellow recalls that "he taught me how to shoot, to swim, and to skate, to play bandy etcetera," bandy being a game much like ice hockey. He had one other interest. With two or three companions he joined the local Thespian Society, held in a neighbourhood hall, where for a small charge they entertained the audience with plays or sketches or declamations. Reportedly John Allan did not approve of his theatrical activities; it may have been too disconcerting a reminder of Poe's dead parents.

Throughout these years, too, Poe continued to write poetry. He claimed to have written some of the poems published in his first book at the age of fourteen; despite his native tendency for exaggeration, there is no reason to question the assertion. His earliest known lines, scrawled on a sheet of John Allan's financial calculations in a neat hand, were composed at the age of fifteen:

> Last night with many cares and toils oppress'd
> Weary . . . I laid me on a couch to rest.

The wistful tone of the couplet is interesting, as is the fact that it was written above Allan's sums of compound interest.

The boy soon found a subject for his romantic melancholia. One of his schoolfellows, Robert Stanard, invited him to his house, where he met Jane Stanard, the thirty-year-old mother, who "took his hand and spoke some gentle and gracious words of welcome." He became smitten, and "returned home in a dream." She might have been his own mother revived.

Jane Stanard has the distinction of being the first motherly young woman to whom Poe became devoted. He had an abiding need for female sympathy and protection. It may be the characteristic of the orphan. In one of his journalistic "marginalia" he wrote later that "the boyish poet-love is indisputably that one of the human sentiments which most nearly realises our dreams of the chastened voluptuousness of heaven."

The pleasure was indeed chastened. Poe possessed an unerring ability to choose frail, or in some way damaged, women, thus revisiting the experience of his fading mother. In the spring of 1824, a year after they had first met, Jane Stanard died insane.

Poe visited her grave in Shockoe Hill Cemetery, and he told a female admirer that he shed tears by the freshly dug earth. All his life he liked to wander through cemeteries. Death and beauty were, in his imagination, inextricably and perpetually associated. "No more" was his favourite phrase. The secret chambers and the mouldering mansions, in which his fictions loved to dwell, are to be construed as those of the mind or of the grave.

He had a more immediate concern for the dead; however. He told a friend, John Hamilton Mackenzie, that "the most horrible thing he could imagine as a boy was to feel

an ice-cold hand laid upon his face in a pitch dark room
when alone at night." That was not his only fantasy. He
feared that he might awake in semi-darkness, only to find
an evil face staring closely at him. He became so afraid of
his own imagined horrors that he would keep his head beneath the sheets until he practically suffocated himself. He
seems to have taken a perverse delight in frightening himself, as well as others. Even in later life he admitted to a
dislike of the dark. Here can be found the origins of his
obsession with death, or deathlike states. Before his twen-
tieth year he wrote a significant couplet:

> I could not love except where Death
> Was mingling his with Beauty's breath.

Yet soon enough he found another thwarted and difficult love. He always said that he was "devoted" to Fanny
Allan, although that attachment had not precluded his at-
traction to Jane Stanard. The love and comfort of one
woman were not enough for him. In the year of Mrs.
Stanard's death he met, and became attached to, a fifteen-
year-old girl. Elmira Royster lived in a house opposite
Poe's school, and so the possibilities of chance encounter
were immense. Under the supervision of the girl's parents,
they met in the parlour of Royster House; she played the
piano, and he sang and played the flute. He made a sketch
of her that survives only in a copy.

She recalled the young Poe remonstrating with her for
her friendship with one young woman whom he consid-

ered to be "unladylike." "He had strong prejudices," she said after his death. "Hated anything coarse and unrefined." She described his grand manner, and his slight shyness in company. He was already growing into the model of a Southern gentleman, but he was not in the conventional mould. Elmira, or "Myra" as he used to call her, recorded that he was "very enthusiastic and impulsive" but that "his general manner was sad."

That sadness had to do with domestic unhappiness. All was not well in the Allan household. Frances Allan may have been exhibiting some of the symptoms of consumption that carried her to the grave five years later. But there were more immediate discontents. Poe and John Allan had begun to quarrel. It is possible that Allan reminded his young charge that he was in effect an object of charity. In November 1824, Allan wrote to Poe's older brother, Henry, that Edgar "does nothing & seems quite miserable, sulky and ill-tempered to all the Family. How we have acted to produce this is beyond my conception . . ." He added that Edgar "possesses not a Spark of affection for us, not a particle of gratitude for all my care and kindness towards him." This would be a complaint about Poe in later years. He could not bring himself to appear humble to anyone or thankful for anything.

In the same letter to Henry Poe, Allan refers to "your poor Sister, Rosalie," who was living with the Mackenzies in Richmond, and writes that "at least She is half your sister & God forbid dear Henry that We should visit upon the living the Errors & frailties of the dead." The meaning of "half your sister" is clear enough. Allan supposed that Rosalie had a different father and that she was, as a consequence, illegitimate. If Allan mentioned this to Henry Poe, he would no doubt have suggested it to Edgar. For a boy who seems to have held his mother in particular reverence, this would have been unpardonable. Poe's hatred of anything "unrefined" has been noticed. What could be more coarse than to accuse his mother of bearing the child of a man who was not her husband?

How did the argument develop? Poe knew of Allan's illegitimate children, living in Richmond, and may have ascribed Frances Allan's weakened health to that cause. If then he upbraided Allan for siring illegitimate offspring, what more natural rejoinder from Allan than that Poe's own mother was guilty of a similar sin? This is the most likely to have been the primary cause of an increasingly bitter conflict. Poe was heard on several occasions wishing that he could escape from the Allan household and thus make his own way in the world. He expressed the desire to the Mackenzies, Rosalie's guardians, that he might run away to sea.

. . .

He did not go to sea. He attended university instead.

In February 1826, at the age of sixteen, he was enrolled at the new University of Virginia in Charlottesville. The cornerstone had been laid nine years previously, but the establishment had been in operation for only a year. Its founder and guiding spirit, Thomas Jefferson, had wished "to develop the reasoning faculties of our youth, enlarge their minds, cultivate their morals," in which ambitions he was not wholly successful. Poe was lodged at number thirteen in the West Range of the new buildings, on the west side of a central lawn, where he roomed alone. Roused by a servant at 5:30 each morning, he began his first classes at 7:00 a.m. in the Schools of Ancient Languages and of Modern Languages. He proved to be a model pupil, adept at translation from Latin as well as Italian. At the end of the year he was recorded as "excelling" in the senior Latin class and the senior French class. He said in a letter to John Allan that he expected to perform well in end of term examinations "if I don't get frightened," an indication of the nervous anxiety that seems to have been his constant companion. He became secretary of the debating club, and was preeminent in the gymnastic exercises of running and jumping.

One fellow student remembered "a sad, melancholy face always, and even a smile, for I don't remember his ever having laughed heartily, seemed to be forced." No one ever really knew him well. He was too defensive, or too proud, to encourage intimacy. He would also "put himself under the influence" of drink in order to "quiet the excessive nervous excitability under which he laboured." The drink in question is likely to have been the ubiquitous "peach [brandy] and honey," a sweet if lethal concoction. This is the first reference to his partiality for alcohol. It is significant that it should have manifested itself at such a relatively early age. He was born, not made, a drinker.

Another fellow student recalls that "Poe's passion for strong drink was as marked and as peculiar as that for cards." Poe loved gambling. When he and a local clerk vied over the purchase of an edition of William Hogarth's prints, Poe proposed that they gamble for the book with dice. Poe lost. He played cards endlessly, often losing large sums of money. In such matters, according to a contemporary, he "plunged with a recklessness of nature which acknowledged no restraint." This "recklessness" was apparent in later life, too, with his increasingly heavy drinking and his sometimes extreme behaviour. Yet it was accompanied, at university, by a steady attention to his studies.

His life at university should in any case be seen in context. The young gentlemen of Virginia did not necessarily obey Thomas Jefferson's injunctions, at least in terms of moral cultivation. There were frequent fist fights, and most students owned a pistol that was readily drawn and fired. The culture of the South still harboured the traditions of the duelling code. Some students came from rich plantation families, and were accompanied by slaves. Some arrived with horses or with hunting dogs. There were drunken forays into the local towns, and inveterate gambling. Poe was not unique in his weaknesses. But he was unusual in not being able to pay for them. He appealed to Allan for money, who sent too little of that commodity too late.

Allan was generally parsimonious in his provisions for the young Poe. In one letter Poe calculated the expenses of life at the university, including board and tuition, at $350 per annum. Allan had dispatched him to Charlottesville with $110 in his pocket. As a result Poe had enrolled in only two of the three schools open to him, thus saving $15. Allan sent him further sums, but they were never enough to allow him to pay his bills. They were certainly insufficient to cover his gambling debts, and according to Poe's complaint he "was immediately regarded in the light of a beggar." There was no apparent reason for Allan's lack of generosity. Only the year before, Allan had inherited a large estate from the will of a wealthy Scottish relative who had also emigrated to America.

It is not surprising that Allan harboured contradictory feelings towards his surrogate son. At a later date Poe himself characterised his foster father to a friend "as a man of gross & brutal temperament though *indulgent to him* at times & at *times* profusely lavish in the matter of money—at others, penurious and parsimonious." It seems likely that Allan came increasingly to resent his young charge. Poe had already appeared to him, as he had to others, arrogant and unthankful. Poe may even have assumed that Allan's wealth would one day be bequeathed to him. This would have been the most hazardous assumption of all.

. . .

When Poe returned to Richmond at the end of 1826, Allan refused to finance any further period of study. Despite dunning letters from the young Poe's creditors, he also refused to pay any more of the debts, which amounted to some $2,000. Poe had expected to spend two years at the university; he would not have acquired a degree in the modern sense, but it would have been formally recorded that he had completed certain courses. He had an immoderate thirst for reading, but any future world of learning was now foreclosed. He told Allan in a subsequent letter that "in a moment of caprice you have blasted my hope." It was a bitter homecoming in another sense: he learned that his letters to Elmira Royster had been kept from her by her father, and that she was about to be married to another man. There were frequent and sharp arguments between Allan and Poe. Any residual love between foster father and foster son had disappeared.

In the middle of March 1827, Poe left the Allan household forever. He went to the Courthouse Tavern, from where he wrote to his surrogate father that "I have heard you say (when you little thought I was listening, and therefore must have said it in earnest) that you had no affection for me." He added that his guardian "was continually upbraiding me with eating the bread of Idleness." He also objected to being under "the complete authority of the blacks," by which he meant that the slaves had adopted their master's manner and attitude towards him. He asked for his trunk, containing his clothes; he was determined to travel north, where in one of the great cities he might earn enough money to complete his studies at university.

But then, in a letter written on the following day, he declared that "I am in the greatest necessity, not having tasted food since Yesterday morning. I have no where to sleep at night, but roam about the Streets—I am nearly exhausted . . ." This is the piteous tone that he would adopt in much of his later correspondence. Allan wrote on the back, "Pretty letter."

. . .

Four days later Edgar Allan Poe was on a coal vessel to Boston. He was on his way back to the place of his birth. It must have been a surprise, after the casual languor of Richmond, to find himself in a city that prided itself on plain living and high thinking. Boston was a city of red brick and white wood. The principal sources of delight were the church and the lecture hall. There were no slaves. The citizens of Boston got up earlier and worked harder than the people of Richmond.

It was not easy, however, for a penniless and failed student to obtain employment in Boston. There are reports of Poe working in a wholesale merchandise house on the waterfront, and even of trying his hand at casual journalism. His first attempt to make his way in the world had foundered. He had no money, and in his desperation he decided to enlist.

Allan wrote to Poe's sister, Rosalie, that "Edgar has

gone to Sea to seek his own fortunes," but in fact he was to be found much closer to home. On 26 May he visited Castle Island in Boston Harbor and, under the assumed name of Edgar A. Perry (Perry had been the name before his own in the entrance records of the university), he enlisted in the United States Army for the next five years. He gave his age as twenty-two, rather than the actual eighteen. Minors were accepted into the Army, so there was no practical reason for him to lie: he just wanted to disappear, and to lose the burden of his identity. In any case, lying came naturally to him.

CHAPTER FOUR

The Soldier

It was not altogether a surprising or even unexpected decision. As a boy he had been appointed lieutenant in the Richmond Junior Volunteers, and at university, too, he had chosen to take part in a course of training in military drill. He needed the constraints of a formal order, no doubt as a counterweight to his pronounced "recklessness." He deliberately sought restraint. He required external discipline in order to balance the miseries and longings of his private nature.

That nature, however, was expressed in an enduring form. During his months in Boston he had become acquainted with an eighteen-year-old printer, Calvin Thomas, who had agreed to publish a selection of Poe's poems. So in the early summer of 1827 fifty copies of *Tamerlane and Other Poems*, written by "a Bostonian," came off Thomas's press. It included poems that Poe had been writing for the last four or five years, comprising the title poem and a number of shorter poems. They evince a strong sense of form, cadence, and metre, equally balanced with a powerful inner mood of mournfulness and introspection. "Tamerlane" itself is a monody on the delights and dangers of ambition, couched in seventeen melancholy stanzas filled with pride and resentment, self-disgust and disillusion. In a preface to the volume Poe claimed that "failure will not at all influence him [Poe] in a resolution already adopted"; that resolution was none other than his aspiration to poetic greatness. His attempt to disarm criticism succeeded admirably. There were no reviews, and only two pre-publication notices, of *Tamerlane*.

When the volume appeared, the young poet was busily engaged in artillery practice. As soon as he had enlisted he had been assigned to duty in an artillery battery off Boston Harbor. Six months later he was moved to Fort Moultrie on Sullivan's Island off the coast of South Carolina; from there, after a further year, he was moved to Fortress Monroe on the tip of the Virginia peninsula. His regimen in these establishments was unchanging, with a wake-up call at 5:30 introducing a day that included infantry drill and exercises at the guns. His own conduct was a model of military discipline. He worked as an assistant and company clerk in the quartermaster's department before being promoted through the various noncommissioned grades. His superiors considered him to be "exemplary in his deportment" and "highly worthy of confidence." Then at the beginning of 1829 he was appointed regimental sergeant major at Fortress Monroe, the

highest rank to which he could aspire. It is perhaps difficult to imagine the author of "The Raven" and "The Fall
of the House of Usher" in uniform. Yet it is an aspect of
Poe's life, and character, that cannot be overlooked. Just as
he could express his passionate and morbid nature in
verses that are strictly controlled, so he could define himself in terms of rigid military identity.

By the time of his promotion to sergeant major, however, he had already had enough of army life. He did not
wish to serve the remaining three and a half years of his
enlistment, and petitioned his commanding officer,
Lieutenant Howard, for release from uniform. He must
also have revealed his true identity, because Howard acqui-
esced on condition that Poe—no longer "Perry"—was
reconciled with John Allan. Howard then wrote to Allan,
only to be sent the reply that Poe "had better remain as he
is until the termination of his enlistment." The fact that
Poe was in the army at all must have come as an unwelcome surprise to Allan. But he showed no remorse at effectively driving him away from home. So on 1 December
1828, Poe wrote him a letter stating that "I could not help
thinking that you believed me degraded & disgraced" by
service in the army; he assured him that "at no period of
my life, have I regarded myself with deeper satisfaction—
or did my heart swell with more honourable pride." He
took pride, among other things, in his capacity for self-
discipline. But he did not wish to waste "the prime of my
life" in further service. That life had only just begun. "I
feel that within me which will make me fulfil your highest

wishes," he added. ". . . I must either conquer or die—succeed or be disgraced." In a final paragraph he sent his love to "Ma," and expressed the hope that his "wayward disposition" would not disappoint her.

He received no reply from Allan, and wrote to him again three weeks later in a more clamant manner imploring, "My father do not throw me aside as *degraded* . . . If you determine to abandon me—here take farewell—Neglected, I will be doubly ambitious." The slightly histrionic tone is in accord with much of his later correspondence. Allan still remained silent. A month passed. Then, at the beginning of February, Poe tried another approach. He asked Allan to assist him in obtaining a cadet's appointment at West Point, the academy for the training of officers in the American army, which would then expedite "an honourable and highly successful course in my own country." There is no doubt that he was serious about his application. Completion of the course at West Point would allow him to become an officer in the army; it would grant him a measure of financial independence as well as much needed social status. His enlistment as a common soldier might otherwise have left him, as he put it, "degraded & disgraced."

His letter arrived at Richmond in a most unhappy time. Frances Allan was dying and, in the final stages of what a local newspaper described as a "lingering and painful" illness, she asked to see the young Poe to hold and kiss him for the last time, but, if she died before he could reach her, she requested that her foster son have the opportunity of seeing her body before she was buried.

On the day of Frances Allan's death at the end of February, Poe was still on the muster roll of his regiment. John Allan had left it to the last minute.

Poe heard of the death on 1 March and left on the afternoon stage from Norfolk to Richmond. When he arrived, on the following day, Fanny had already been buried. His surrogate father had purchased for Poe a suit of mourning clothes. In that dress he visited the new grave in Shockoe cemetery. He collapsed upon the spot, and was helped back into the carriage by the family's slaves. "*Your* love I never valued," he wrote to John Allan at a later date, when all seemed hopeless, "but she I believed loved me as her own child." Another mother had been taken away from him, a double orphanhood that increased the burden of his woe. It is worth noting that the Shockoe cemetery was the resting place of Jane Stanard, his schoolfriend's young mother to whom Poe had been devoted.

His relationship with John Allan entered a new phase. It seems that his guardian had been softened by the death of Fanny, and that the presence of Poe was no longer objectionable to him. Poe related his plans to enroll at West Point, and he obtained Allan's consent. The way was now open for him to be honourably discharged. He left Richmond a week later, and on his return to Fortress Monroe he sent a letter to Allan as "My dear Pa" rather than as the "Dear Sir" of his previous correspondence.

. . .

At the end of March the process of discharging Poe began. He was obliged to find a substitute for his service, and informed the colonel of the garrison that he was "one of a family of orphans whose unfortunate parents were the victims of the conflagration of the Richmond theatre," a flagrant lie designed to cover up what he considered to be his dubious origins. The explanation was accepted, however, and in the following month he returned to Richmond.

The path to West Point, however, was not easy. In the first weeks of his return Poe set about gaining political referees to bolster his application, among them a local major and the representative in Congress for his district. Allan must have materially assisted him, but wrote a reference that was curiously impersonal: "Frankly, sir," he wrote to the Secretary of War, "I do declare that he is no relation to me whatever . . . but I do request your kindness to aid this youth in the promotion of his future prospects." Allan did have some interest, however, in dispatching Poe to West Point; he would be out of the house and, more important, no longer a financial burden.

Poe submitted a formal application to West Point in May and, with a gift from Allan of fifty dollars in his pocket, travelled to Washington in order to present in person his letters of recommendation to the Secretary of War. He learned that there were some forty-seven candidates already on the list of appointments, but that it still might be possible for him to enroll in September. He then travelled thirty miles north to Baltimore. He wanted to be reunited with his older brother, Henry, who had been living with General Poe and his family since infancy; this visit would also allow Poe to become acquainted with his paternal relatives. Now that his substitute family had been fragmented, he was happy to be embraced by what might be called his true relations. It was also possible that some erstwhile colleague of General Poe might help his enlistment at West Point.

Baltimore was the third largest city in the United States, but still at the very beginning of its fortunes. The Baltimore & Ohio Railroad had just been completed. The Patapsco river-front was lined with warehouses. Baltimore was becoming a centre for manufacturing as well as for shipping, an energetic and serious city with broad streets and a skyline made memorable by buildings and churches. Two years before, John Quincy Adams had called it "Monument City." The earliest photographs depict the busy area of the port, behind which, in the distance, can be seen the Basilica of the Assumption, the steeples of Saint Paul's Episcopal church and the German Reformed Church, and the Washington Monument. It was also the first city of slavery for those travelling south. In that sense, at least, Poe felt at home.

Poe had a further purpose in coming to Baltimore. He was eager to publish another volume of poetry. He had the abiding dream of literary success but, in addition, he possessed an almost visceral need to be seen by the eyes of the world. He yearned for distinction. Soon after his arrival he took the steamboat to Philadelphia and presented his manuscript of poems to a likely publisher, Carey, Lea & Carey. Mr. Lea seemed to be interested in the volatile and no doubt voluble young poet, and promised to study the manuscript carefully with a view to publication. Much encouraged, Poe returned to Baltimore. A few weeks later Lea sent him a standard and disheartening letter. The poems might be published if the publishers were guaranteed against loss.

Poe had very little money of his own. So he wrote to Allan, asking him to furnish the financial subsidy for the book. This was a surprising and perhaps foolish action. Nothing was more calculated to arouse Allan's anger. He had considered Poe to be on the way to a distinguished military career—but here the young man was, pursuing an insecure and even reprehensible destiny. Poetry was not at a premium in early-nineteenth-century America. Allan scribbled at the end of Poe's letter that he had replied, "strongly censuring his conduct & refusing any aid."

Allan had meanwhile been supporting Poe at the least possible cost. He sent his young charge a further fifty dollars in the summer of 1829, upon which sum he was supposed to live for the next three months. It amounted to a daily allowance of some fifty-three cents. Poe decided to move out of lodging houses and into the home of his relatives, situated in the business district, "down-town" from the wealthier and more fashionable quarter.

General Poe was dead, survived by his widow; in her

little house in Mechanics Row, Milk Street, was also Maria Clemm, Poe's aunt, together with her small daughter, Virginia. And here lived Poe's brother, Henry. It was not necessarily a happy family: old Mrs. Poe was paralysed, and Mrs. Clemm also in a poor state of health; Henry was dying of tuberculosis, and according to Poe, "entirely given up to drink & unable to help himself, much less me." There was real poverty in Mechanics Row, where Poe experienced a life very different from that of the Allan household in Richmond. Yet his entrance into the family marked a decisive change in his life. He became attached to Maria Clemm, and to her young daughter. In succeeding years these two women would become the lodestones of his life, the harbour into which he crept from the wild waves of the world.

. . .

Poe's poetic ambitions left everything in doubt. Allan was now not at all convinced that the young man was serious about a military career, and accused him of shiftiness and prevarication. He was also enraged by Poe's requests for more money, in order to procure a substitute for his service at Fortress Monroe. Poe wrote that, while in Baltimore, one of his cousins had stolen money from his pockets. It must have seemed to Allan that his demands would never cease. In a letter to him of this period, Poe declared that "I would have returned home immediately but for the words in your letter 'I am not particularly anxious to see you.' "

He was happy to remain in Baltimore for a specific reason. He had retrieved the manuscript of his poetry from Carey, Lea & Carey, offering it instead to the Baltimore publishing firm of Hatch and Dunning. To his delight, it was accepted. *Al Aaraaf, Tamerlane and Minor Poems* by Edgar A. Poe was published in December 1829. In some respects it is a reprise of *Tamerlane*, published two years earlier. But there are many new poems, among them "Al Aaraaf" itself, which owes as much to Milton as to the Romantics. The newly published poems once more evince Poe's mastery of form and cadence; his characteristics are those of intensity aligned with indefiniteness, of lyricism melting into morbidity.

There was one particular person to whom he had yet to prove himself. Poe wrote to his foster father announcing the publication, and one of the publishers, Mr. Dunning, promised to present a copy of the volume to Allan in person.

For the first time, Poe received praise for his accomplishment. John Neal, the editor of the *Yankee and Boston Literary Gazette*, having been sent some poems in advance of publication, wrote that if he "would but do himself justice he might make a beautiful and perhaps a magnificent poem." Poe was always immensely susceptible to praise, and wrote a reply to Neal in which he stated that "I am young—not yet twenty—*am* a poet—if deep worship of all beauty can make me *one* . . ." He added that "I have no father—nor mother." This insistence upon his status as an orphan was another way of gaining sympathy and attention.

Poe probably wished to stay in Baltimore, but he was miserably poor. Poetry could not save him from destitution. There is a record of his selling one of Mrs. Clemm's slaves in December 1829, but in the early months of 1830 he was forced to return to the Allan household. There was nowhere else to go except to Richmond. There he was tolerated rather than welcomed, with the clear understanding that he would be departing for West Point in a relatively short time. The atmosphere in the house was not pleasant, and in a letter to Sergeant Graves, one of his creditors, he confessed that "I have tried to get the money for you from Mr. A[llan] a dozen times—but he always shuffles me off." He also remarked that "Mr. A is not very often sober," an accusation that would later rebound against him.

. . .

Poe left Richmond in the middle of May 1830. He told Allan in a subsequent letter that "when I parted from you—at the steamboat, I knew that I should never see you again." He stopped at Baltimore for a day or so, and then went on to West Point. The United States Military Academy, built on a green plain, on high ground some two hundred feet above the Hudson River in New York State, had been established in 1804 for the training of officers. Charles Dickens in his *American Notes* described it as a "beautiful place: the fairest among the fair and lovely highlands of the river: shut in by deep green heights and ruined forts, and looking down upon the distant town of Newburgh, along a glittering path of sunlit water, with here and there a skiff . . ."

Poe was lodged with three other cadets at 28 South Barracks, and was paid an allowance of $16 per month. The young poet wore a uniform of blue cloth, with a single-breasted coat; his cap sported a cockade; and he wore his sword in a frog belt under his coat. Reveille was at sunrise. Breakfast was followed by lectures; then at 4:00 p.m. there were various exercises and drills before the cadets were given their supper in a large mess hall and sent back to quarters for further study. The lights were dimmed at 9:30 p.m. There was little time for leisure.

There are contrary reports about Poe from his contemporaries. One cadet recalled him as "a slovenly, heedless boy, very eccentric, inclined to dissipation, and, of course, preferred making verses to solving equations." This does not ring altogether true. Poe was never "slovenly" in dress or demeanour. Another cadet more plausibly described him as "shy, proud, sensitive, and unsociable with the other cadets. He spent more time in reading than in study . . ." Yet his study, brief though it may have been, was sufficient. He was always a quick learner. He attended the classes in French and mathematics; at the general examination in the following year, he was placed seventeenth in mathematics and third in French. He cannot have been altogether unsociable, either, since the cadets learned from him some interesting details about his past life. He told them that he had graduated from a college in England, had become one of the crew on a whaler, had visited South America as well as the East. He was a congenital fabulist, a mendacity that suggests insecurity and pride in equal measure.

The most complete description of him comes from one of his roommates, Cadet Gibson, who recorded "a worn, weary discontented look, not easily forgotten by those who were intimate with him. Poe was easily fretted by any jest at his expense . . . Very early in his brief career at the Point he established a high reputation for genius, and poems and squibs of local interest were daily issued from Number 28 . . ." Gibson also added that "I never heard him speak in praise of any English writer living or dead." On occasions Poe accused his contemporaries of plagiarism or, even worse, bad grammar. He always would be scornful of those who might rival him. He also had a reputation for "hoaxes" or practical jokes, a habit he was never really able to break in later life. These jokes tended to be of an eerie or bloody kind. On one occasion he insisted that the corpse of a strangled gander was in fact the severed head of an unpopular teacher. He enjoyed scaring his companions. In this respect, too, he would not altogether change.

Poe soon became weary of West Point life. One contemporary states that within "a few weeks" he "seemed to lose interest in his studies and to be disheartened and discouraged." This was not the life he had imagined for himself. He was also in debt again. So he set about resigning.

Unfortunately, such a course could not be pursued without the permission of a parent or guardian; Poe wrote to John Allan asking for his consent, and was "flatly refused." It was clear to Allan that Poe had returned to a capricious and wayward life.

Something else had happened in the Allan household, however, which rendered Allan even less sympathetic than before. He had married again, and had before him the prospect of legitimate children. Why should he any longer help to sustain a scapegrace? The gossip that eventually reached Allan only added to the impression that Poe was malicious as well as mendacious; he had described his surrogate father to Sergeant Graves as "not very often sober."

Allan, in a letter now lost, asked Poe not to trouble him with any "further communication." In his reply Poe rehearsed the litany of complaints against his erstwhile guardian, and justified his previous behaviour at the University of Virginia on the grounds that "it was my crime to have no one on Earth who cared for me, or loved me." He seemed to have forgotten Fanny Allan for the moment, but the note of anguish and self-pity was never far from the surface. He added that "my future life (which thank God will not endure long) must be passed in indigence and sickness. I have no energy left, nor health." This is the first indication that the manifest strength and healthiness of his boyhood years had now left him forever, and it may be related to another observation of his roommate, Gibson, that "I don't think he was ever intoxicated while at the Academy, but he had already acquired the more dangerous habit of constant drinking." Yet Poe was determined. In the absence of express permission from his guardian, he would obtain his discharge from West Point by other means. He told Allan, "I shall neglect my studies and duties at the institution." On the back of this letter Allan scrawled, "I do not think the Boy has one good quality . . . I cannot believe a word he writes."

The subject of Poe's drinking has often been invoked as the cause of all his misfortunes. There is no doubt that he drank often and that he drank heavily; but the theory that he became intoxicated after only one drink does not stand up to scrutiny. He often had "just the one" and did not become inebriated. On the other hand, there are many reports of his drinking through the afternoon, through the night, or even through the week. And he did become very drunk indeed, with the urgent necessity of being rescued or assisted home. The police were sometimes called. He did not drink for the pleasure of it—there are reports of him downing a glass of wine or spirits in one gulp, as if he were in the thrall of some unconquerable need. Once he had started, he found it difficult to stop. As one friend put it, "if he took but one glass of weak wine or beer the Rubicon of the cup was passed with him, and it almost always ended in excess and sickness." Drink absolved him from fears of the future. Drink allowed him to forget his poverty and his sense of failure. Drink tempered his nervous disposition, and lent him confidence. Drink may perhaps have helped him to regain some state of infantile bliss, freed from the constraints and difficulties of the world. Yet, when he became drunk, he was aggressive and peremptory and ferocious. Since both his father and brother were heavy drinkers, there may have been an inherited disposition or tendency. Nevertheless he could abstain from drink for long periods without any noticeable ill effects. Yet there is no doubt that frequent intoxication severely damaged his physical, as well as his mental, health. From the time of West Point forward, he would never be wholly well.

His plan to leave the academy, through dereliction of duty, succeeded admirably. From the beginning of 1831 he absented himself from military exercises, and refused to attend the mandatory church services. He did not report for parades or for guard duty. At the end of January he was brought before a court martial, where he was charged with "gross neglect of duty" and "disobedience of orders." He pleaded guilty to all charges, and was therefore judged as such. Edgar Allan Poe was dismissed from the service of the United States and, on 19 February, took his place aboard a steamboat bound for New York. He told Allan that he had embarked with "no cloak" to protect him from the winter weather. That was not strictly true. He kept his cadet's overcoat for the rest of his life.

CHAPTER FIVE

The Journalist

So Poe came to New York. He rented a poor lodging somewhere near Madison Square, but almost at once fell ill with an ear infection and a bad cold. The life of New York was in every respect different from that of Richmond and even of Baltimore. He had grown up in what was still primarily an agricultural society, with various gradations in rank and standing; he had come to a city that was beginning its industrial and mercantile career, with all the energetic and levelling forces unleashed by such enterprise. It was faster, and harder, than any city he had ever known. Henry James described it as "the old liquor-scented, heated-looking city," a city of pigs and horses, a city of flash money. In the year of Poe's arrival, the first street car made its way along Fourth Avenue.

The city was growing slowly and surely northward; with its seed in the old port neighbourhood, it had reached by the early 1830s the approximate point of what is now

Canal Street. Above that line were small shanty towns of Irish squatters as well as the dwellings of labourers and builders clearing the ground for further construction. There were also large farms and farmhouses planted in what was once virgin territory. Now the smell of brick-dust was in the air as the growth of the city increased in momentum. It was a noisy, thriving, and sometimes bewildering place. Broadway and the Bowery were already in existence, exhibiting some of the characteristics that until recently they still possessed. Broadway was the home of retail shops and theatres, while the Bowery led a more penurious existence as the haven for slums and saloon bars.

From his sickroom, two days after his arrival, Poe told Allan that "I have no money—no friends . . . I shall never rise from my bed." Allan did not reply to this distressing letter, but he did preserve it. At a later date he wrote upon it, "it is now upwards of 2 years since I received the above precious relict of the Blackest Heart & deepest ingratitude alike destitute of honour & principle every day of his life has only served to confirm his debased nature." He was not, in other words, to be reconciled to Poe, however miserable the young man's circumstances. In the absence of any reply, Poe became desperate. He even wrote to the superintendent of West Point, from which he had just been dishonourably discharged, and asked for a reference. He professed a wish to join the Polish army. The superintendent, Colonel Thayer, did not reply.

Poe remained in New York for only three months. His finances were, to say the least, uncertain. He had taken up a subscription among his fellow cadets at West Point, for the publication of a book of poems. They expected a volume of satires, in the style with which he had entertained them before, but they were to be disappointed. In April 1831, *Poems by Edgar A. Poe* was published, dedicated to "The U.S. Corps of Cadets." But it was not written with young soldiers in mind. Poe included new poems, such as "Israfel," "To Helen," and "The Doomed City," poems that confirmed his imaginative interest in forlorn and mournful introspection; it was as if he sensed that he would never be happy on this earth. There is a tendency to apostrophise death as a place of repose and consolation. There are other passages of poetry which also offer remarkable intimations of his future writing:

> Be silent in that solitude
> Which is not loneliness, for then
> The spirits of the dead who stood
> In life before thee are again
> In death around thee, and their will
> Shall overshadow thee: be still.

This is fine writing, at once forceful and melodic with a sure sense of cadence and an unforced immediacy of meaning. It is one aspect of Poe's misfortune on earth that the quality of his poetry was never recognised in his lifetime. He was in a literal sense doomed to be misunderstood. He would not publish another volume of poetry for fourteen years.

He wrote a preface for the volume, entitled "Letter to Mr.——," in which he stated the poetic creed by which he would be guided for the rest of his life. "A poem in my opinion," he wrote, "is opposed to a work of science by having, for its *immediate* object, pleasure, not truth; to romance by having, for its object, an *indefinite* instead of a *definite* pleasure." He went on to claim that poetry is concerned "with *in*definite sensations, to which end music is an *essential*, since the comprehension of sweet sound is our most indefinite conception." This is one of the first statements of the belief in art for art's sake that, through Poe's agency, would have such a profound effect upon the course of nineteenth-century French poetry; his connection of poetry and music here predates Walter Pater's similar sentiments by forty-six years.

. . .

Since life in New York had become insupportable, in May he travelled back to his Baltimore relations. Life in Mechanics Row was no less poor and disorderly than before, but the situation was rendered even more hopeless by the spectacle of his brother dying of consumption. It was the family disease. Poe shared the rear attic room with the invalid, where, in August, Henry Poe died of "intemperance" at the age of twenty-four. In a letter written two years earlier, Poe had confessed that "there can be no tie more strong than that of brother for brother—it is not so much that they love one another as that they both love the same parent." The singular parent here can only mean his mother. In the death of Henry, another part of Eliza Poe had also died.

His aunt, Maria Clemm, an ambiguous figure, was the one who tried to sustain the household throughout this difficult period. She was adept at eking out small means, whether in terms of stitching and sewing or in terms of food and cooking; she kept her family, of which Poe soon became an integral part, together at all costs. Poe came to depend upon her wholly, for all the necessities of his life. But she inevitably gained a reputation as something of a beggar or cadger. She was forty-one when Poe joined the household and was considered to be somewhat masculine in appearance, with a large forehead and a firm chin. And, for obscure reasons, she was given the nickname of "Muddy."

Maria Clemm's daughter, Virginia, was nine years old when Poe came back to Baltimore. Poe called her "Sis" or "Sissie." She was childlike, or doll-like, with a very pale complexion. She was a little plump, but had the large eyes and raven hair to which Poe was instinctively attracted.

He called her "Sissie" even after he married her.

. . .

In his first months in Baltimore he tried to gain work as an usher in a local school, but was turned down. In his financial distress he decided as a last resort to live by his pen.

He began writing stories, and may even have tried his hand at "penny a line" journalism in the provincial newspapers. But he was always desperately poor. In November he wrote to Allan telling him that "I was arrested eleven days ago for a debt which I never expected to have to pay" and asked for money. Two weeks later Maria Clemm seconded his appeal with a letter of her own, in which she claimed that "he is extremely distressed at your refusal to assist him." There is, however, no record of Poe's arrest or imprisonment at this time. If it were in fact an elaborate subterfuge to acquire funds from Allan, then it is clear that Mrs. Clemm was deep in Poe's confidence. He wrote two further letters to his erstwhile guardian at the end of the year. In the first he stated that "sickness and misfortune have left me not a shadow of pride. I own that I am miserable and unworthy of notice, but do not leave me to perish without leaving me still one resource." Two weeks later he wrote again to Allan, imploring him for aid, "for the sake of the love you bore me when I sat upon your knee and called you father."

At the beginning of the following year, Poe received a belated gift of twenty dollars from his guardian. It would keep him from starving. There are some reports that Poe travelled back to Richmond in the summer of this year, either to confront or to placate Allan. But there is no firm evidence for such a visit.

. . .

In January 1832, the *Saturday Courier* of Philadelphia had the distinction of printing Poe's first published tale.

It was entitled "Metzengerstein," and was written in the style of a Germanic tale of horror. During that year the same magazine would print four other stories by Poe, "Duke de L'Omelette," "A Tale of Jerusalem," "A Decided Loss," and "The Bargain Lost." Although these are tales of the horrid or of the supernatural, they are couched in a satirical or parodic vein. He had been reading journals such as *Blackwood's Magazine,* and had quickly learned how to couch a tale of "sensation." But this was not for him the serious work of poetry; it was a way of earning a living, and something of his scorn is conveyed in these adept but deeply ironic exercises in the flesh-creeping genre. Yet, in the garret in Mechanics Row, he had found his true vocation.

We may take the first published of them, "Metzengerstein," as representative. It is a high-spirited and engaging, and at the same time a well-calculated, story of horror and metempsychosis set in Hungary. It concerns the young Baron Metzengerstein who, having lost both of his parents in quick succession, enters upon a stupendous inheritance; here we may, if we wish, see the stirrings of wish fulfilment. In his dissipated career, however, it seems that there are already hints "of morbid melancholy, and hereditary illhealth." The baron burns down the stables of a particular enemy but then, apparently in retribution, a horse stitched within a tapestry of his apartments comes alive with its "sepulchral and disgusting teeth." Eventually the baron rides upon it to his doom. It is all very strident and colourful, and of course not to be taken seriously—except for the fact that its purpose was to thrill and to surprise a large audience of somewhat credulous readers. This was to become the central paradox of Poe's literary career.

. . .

Poe's life in Baltimore is relatively well documented. He attended the Baltimore Library, where he continued what was essentially a course in self-education, and frequented a bookstore on Calvert Street and an oyster parlour on Pratt Street. He courted a young lady who lived in his neighbourhood, Mary Devereaux, who has left a short description of her young beau. Poe "didn't like trifling and small talk. He didn't like dark-skinned people . . . He had a quick, passionate temper, and was very jealous. His feelings were intense, and he had but little control of them. He was not well balanced; he had too much brain. He scoffed at everything sacred and never went to church . . . He said often that there was a mystery hanging over him he never could fathom." For all its ingenuousness, this sounds like an accurate remembrance. He would quote Burns to her on their rambles through the city and its adjacent hills. "The only thing I had against him," she added, "was that he held his head so high. He was proud and looked down on my uncle whose business did not suit him."

His quick temper and ready passion were evident in one story Mary Devereaux recounted. She tells how, after a lovers' quarrel, she had retreated to her house. Poe followed her, and peremptorily ordered her mother to allow him to see her. On another occasion he is supposed to have "cowhided" her uncle for the offence of sending him a "cutting" letter. This is all highly characteristic of Poe's later, and even more erratic, behaviour. A Baltimore contemporary provides a more objective account. Poe's "figure was remarkably good, and he carried himself erect and well, as one who had been trained to it. He was dressed in black, and his frockcoat was buttoned to the throat, where it met the black stock, then almost universally worn." He would dress in black for the rest of his life. It was his colour.

The publication of his early stories, and the composition of "hack work" which has yet to be discovered in the columns of now defunct local periodicals, did not materially affect his poverty. In April 1833, he wrote another despairing letter to John Allan in which he declared that he was "without friends, without any means, consequently of obtaining employment, I am perishing—absolutely perishing for want of aid . . . For God's sake pity me, and save me from destruction." Allan did not reply. There was no further correspondence between them.

But Poe had not been idle. In the following month he sent a short story to the *New England Magazine*, one of a sequence of narratives that he proposed to publish under the title of "Eleven Tales of the Arabesque." He offered to send the complete works and added, in a postscript, "I am poor."

His fortunes improved in the autumn of 1833, however, after he had submitted various stories for a competition set up by the *Baltimore Saturday Visiter*. A prize of fifty dollars was to be awarded to the best story. The editorial committee of the *Visiter* unanimously decided that "MS Found in a Bottle" was "so far, so very far, superior to anything before us" that the prize had to be given to the young and unknown author. Poe had also submitted a poem, for the poetry prize of twenty-five dollars. He would have won that, too, if the committee had not thought that the benefaction of two prizes was excessive. The story, of a supernatural voyage complete with phantom crew and "chaos of formless water," was published at the beginning of October. It is a variant of the "Flying Dutchman" legend but imbued with Poe's fascination with the maelstrom and the wild abyss.

It was one of the few triumphant moments in Poe's literary career. For the first time he had been afforded recognition. His prospects of fame and fortune had been transformed. On the Sunday and Monday after the award had been announced in the journal, he called upon the members of the editorial committee. One of them, Mr. Latrobe, recalled that "his manner was easy and quiet, and although he came to return thanks for what he regarded as deserving them, there was nothing obsequious in what he said or did." He noted that Poe's "forehead was high, and remarkable for the great development of the temple. This was the characteristic of his head, which you noticed at once, and which I have never forgotten." This was a frequent remark about him—that there was something about his appearance that was indeed unforgettable. He went on to tell Latrobe that he was presently engaged on a story about a voyage by balloon to the moon, and in the course of his explanation "he clapped his hands and stamped with his foot by way of emphasis." Afterwards he laughed and apologised for his "excitability."

One of the other editors whom he met on that Sunday, John P. Kennedy, became his unofficial patron. On a later occasion he recalled to Kennedy "those circumstances of absolute despair in which you found me" and "how great reason I have to be grateful to God and yourself." In a diary written after Poe's death, Kennedy recorded that "I found him in Baltimore in a state of starvation."

Yet Poe now had some reason for hopefulness. In October the *Visiter* announced that "a volume of tales from the pen of Edgar A. Poe" was to be published by subscription. The intended book was to be entitled *Tales of the Folio Club*, and comprised some seventeen stories. Each of these stories was narrated by a member of the club, and there were general critical discussions among them after every contribution. It was a showcase, in other words, for Poe's heterogeneous talents. The stories were, in Poe's words, "of a bizarre and generally whimsical character"; more significantly they were largely designed as satires on a range of literary styles, from the Germanic sensationalism of *Blackwood's Magazine* to the snappy journalistic style currently fashionable. He caricatured writers as diverse as Walter Scott and Thomas Moore, Benjamin Disraeli and Washington Irving. The tales ranged from "The

Spectacles," a story in which the narrator falls in love with his own grandmother, to the necrophiliac "King Pest," and the narrators themselves were given names such as Horribile Dictu and Convolvulus Gondola. It was indeed a convoluted humour, but it is important to note that Poe embarked upon his fictional career as a predominantly satirical writer. There was always a trace of vaudeville in his performance.

Poe's humour was, at the best of times, somewhat laboured. He often verged upon facetiousness, and delighted in what can only be called gallows humour. He only ever approached wit in his scathing reviews of other writers, where an almost Wildean note emerges. His principal gift was for sarcasm, an effortless tone of superiority not unmixed with contempt. He also enjoyed "hoaxing," with accounts of imaginary voyages to the icy regions and of trips to the moon; there is in fact a serious argument that he was "hoaxing" in his tales of horror, deliberately piling the terror onto a gullible public. "The Black Cat" and "The Tell-Tale Heart" are also exercises in burlesque.

. . .

In March 1834 John Allan died and, as Poe expected, left nothing in his will to his erstwhile foster child. Yet anticipation did not necessarily soften the blow. "I am thrown entirely upon my own resources," he told Kennedy, "with no profession, and very few friends." Throughout his life Poe continually complained about friendlessness, as if somehow it emphasised his orphan status. There had been a time when Poe had hoped, or even expected, to receive a large inheritance from his guardian. If Frances Allan had lived, he might have gained the entire estate. But in fact he was consigned to a life of penury and, as always, he harboured grief and resentment at being so unluckily and unnaturally cast away.

In addition the publication of *Tales of the Folio Club* had come to nothing, foundering on the reluctance of publishers to take on a volume of short stories by an American writer. Indigenous writers were at a grave disadvantage during this period. They survived only by taking other professions, such as diplomacy and education, or by relying upon an independent income. The cultural palm was given to the English, but, more important, books from England could be pirated and reprinted at no cost at all. There was no copyright legislation in existence. To pay a native writer, for what could be appropriated free of charge from another country, seemed to many publishers to be an unnecessary expense. So Poe suffered. He was one of the first truly professional writers in American literary history, but he was in a marketplace where none came to buy. It has been estimated that the total income from all of his books, over a period of twenty years, was approximately three hundred dollars.

In the unhappy year of 1834, when Poe was twenty-five, there were reports of his suffering a heart attack, of his being incarcerated in a local jail, and of his being employed for a time as a bricklayer or as a lithographer. None of these stories can be substantiated. It can be confirmed, however, that he applied for a post as schoolteacher in the spring of 1835.

A letter to Kennedy, asking for assistance, survives. Kennedy, still one of the editors of the *Baltimore Saturday Visiter*, invited Poe to dinner, after receiving his letter of solicitation, but Poe had to decline on the very good grounds that he had nothing suitable to wear. He only had the one shabby black suit that he donned on all occasions. Kennedy realised at once the extent of the young man's penury. He gave him clothing, afforded him free access to his table, and even lent him a horse for periodic exercise. He lifted him "from the very verge of despair."

Kennedy performed a further favour for Poe in the spring of 1835. He gave him what Poe called "my first start in the literary world," without which "I should not at this moment be among the living." Kennedy recommended him to the editor of the newly established *Southern Literary Messenger*, Thomas Willis White, whose offices were in Richmond. It was the best possible introduction for an aspiring writer. Kennedy advised White that Poe was "*very* poor," and he counselled the editor to accept articles from the talented young man. Poe sent one of his tales of terror, "Berenice"; it was promptly accepted. Then he entered into a correspondence with White in which he advised the new editor on journalistic principles. He recommended changes in typeface, and also in style. "To be appreciated," he told him, "you must be read." White had criticised aspects of "Berenice" as "too horrible," and Poe admitted the impeachment. But he went on to say that the most successful stories contained "the ludi-crous heightened into the grotesque: the fearful coloured into the horrible: the witty exaggerated into the burlesque: the singular wrought out into the strange and mystical. You may say all this is bad taste." This was Poe's journalis-tic credo, the principles of which he followed for the rest of his writing career. He had an instinctive understanding of what would attract, and hold the attention of, a newly formed reading public. He understood the virtues of terseness and unity of effect; he realised the necessity of sensationalism and of the exploitation of contemporary "crazes." In his lifetime he was sometimes condemned as a mere "Magazinist," but that perilous and badly rewarded profession would be the cradle of his genius.

As a result of Poe's unasked-for advice on editorial matters, White wrote to him in June, 1835, offering him a post on the journal. His acceptance would mean that he would be obliged to move to Richmond. But the prospect of work, and money, triumphed over any local inconve-nience. Poe replied at once, promising his services to the *Southern Literary Messenger* and professing that he was "anx-ious to settle myself" in his hometown. So in the summer of 1835 Poe returned to the scenes of his childhood.

He rented a room in a boarding house and, after a pe-riod of prevarication in which he applied unsuccessfully for a post as a schoolteacher at Richmond Academy, he joined White's periodical at a salary of sixty dollars per month. It was his first prospect of prolonged paid employ-ment. Quite by chance the headquarters of the *Messenger*

were beside the offices of Ellis and Allan, John Allan's erstwhile business, so he was offered daily reminders of his
change of status or what he used to call "caste." He was engaged, after all, in what was essentially hack work. With
White abroad gathering subscriptions, Poe was obliged to
write most of the periodical himself. He contributed book
reviews and squibs and heterogeneous "copy," all against
an advancing deadline; he was also engaged in binding up
and addressing the numbers of each edition. Printer's ink
was the air he breathed. The periodical came out monthly,
at a subscription price of five dollars a year, and comprised
some thirty-two double-columned octavo pages. There
was a great deal of space to fill.

. . .

In August, however, the delicate balance of his nature
was entirely overthrown. Maria Clemm wrote to inform
him that his cousin Neilson Poe was ready to take in and
educate her daughter Virginia at his own expense. There
was already some presumption that Poe would one day
marry Virginia, and he replied with an hysterical communication which opened "I am blinded with tears while writing this letter." In the course of it he declared that "I have
no desire to live and *will not*," while adding that "you know
I love Virginia passionately devotedly." The prospect of
losing another young female, just as he had lost his mother
and Jane Stanard, rendered him almost helpless with grief.
"Oh God have mercy on me. What have I *to live for?*
Among strangers with *not one soul to love me.*" He also en-

closed a letter to Virginia in which he called her "my own sweetest Sissy, my darling little wifey" and implored her not to "break the heart of your cousin. Eddy."

He invited Mrs. Clemm and her daughter to leave Baltimore in order to live with him in Richmond, and lied that he had "procured a sweet little house in a retired situation." The house's "situation" was only in his imagination. He had the propensity of believing that anything he wrote down somehow became true.

There was no immediate resolution to this crisis, and in the following month Poe became deeply melancholic. In a letter from Richmond he told Kennedy that "I am wretched, and know not why." This is an odd admission, since he knew that the reason for his depression lay in the possibility of losing Virginia forever. It can only be attributed to the fact that he was constantly demanding the sympathy of others; he was always desperately in need of love and attention. But he also began drinking heavily. White wrote to one friend that Poe "is unfortunately rather dissipated, and therefore I can place very little reliance upon him." One of the printers in the office of the *Messenger* recalled that "Mr. Poe was a fine gentleman when he was sober. He was ever kind and courtly, and at such times everyone liked him. But when he was drinking he was about one of the most disagreeable men I have ever met."

. . .

In September Poe suddenly vacated his desk. He "flew the track," as White put it; he added that "I should not be at all astonished to hear that he has been guilty of suicide." Poe did not kill himself, however. He returned to Baltimore, where it is surmised that he secretly married Virginia. The evidence for this is uncertain, but it is clear that some arrangement was reached. Marriage may have been the only way of retaining Virginia for himself. Since she was only thirteen years old, some element of secrecy was obviously considered desirable.

At the end of that month he wrote to White, asking to be reinstated at the *Messenger*. White consented on the understanding that Poe would refrain from drinking. "No man is safe who drinks before breakfast," he told him. "No man can do so, and attend to business properly." So Poe had been drinking very deeply indeed. Two or three of his tales from this time, among them "Shadow" and "King Pest," offer visions of men sitting around a table drinking even as death is a guest among them. Their drinking parlours are enclosed and shrouded from view, lit by lamps or torches: it is the nightmare vision of a tavern, where drink and death are part of the same lurid and fitfully lit reality. He had seen such taverns, in New York as well as in Richmond, where a flight of steps from the street led down to a room with a packed dirt floor. It was little more than a converted cellar, with a wooden counter and wooden benches. Poe knew these leprous places very well.

At the beginning of October Poe returned from Baltimore to Richmond. With him he brought Maria Clemm and Virginia. They took rooms in a boarding house, rather than the "sweet little house" he had promised to them. The three of them maintained the appearance of a bachelor cousin, and a mother, caring for a girl. Almost as soon as they arrived Maria Clemm wrote to a relation that "we are entirely dependent on Edgar. He is, indeed, a son to me & has always been so . . ."

White appointed Poe editor of the *Messenger,* retaining his own role as proprietor, and at first he prospered in his new role. He gave up drinking, now that the cause of his unhappiness had been removed, and told Kennedy in a letter that he had "fought the enemy manfully." He went on to state that "my health is better than for years past, my mind is fully occupied, my pecuniary difficulties have vanished, I have a fair prospect of future success . . ."

He had also been writing steadily. Ever since the *Southern Literary Messenger* had published "Berenice," he had contributed other tales and essays to the periodical. The December number, for example, contained "MS Found in a Bottle," an uncompleted drama entitled "Politian," two or three "fillers" and critical reviews of no less than nineteen books. In the previous nine months he had published six new stories, among them "Hans Phaall—A Tale," "Morella," and "King Pest."

His reviews provoked immediate attention, since he brought to them a fine critical mind tempered with satire and mordant wit. The reputations of some of the most fashionable writers of the time did not emerge unscathed from the inflictions of Poe's pen. He was irritable and even savage in his criticisms. His dissatisfaction with the world was part of his dissatisfaction with himself. Jung's remarks about Paracelsus are apposite here: ". . . when one unconsciously works against oneself, the result is impatience, irritability, and an impotent longing to get one's opponent down whatever the means." Poe certainly enjoyed causing trouble, or what he called "kicking up a bobbery," especially when it was at the expense of New York or New England writers. He was already a defiantly Southern writer, or Southern journalist, not at all ready to bow to the literary claims of his Northern neighbours. He also wanted reputation; he wanted fame; he needed to make an impression, at whatever cost.

The journalism has passed, but the stories survive. "Berenice" in a sense sets the tone for many that followed. It is both morbid and macabre, with more than a dash of sensationalism to season the characteristic mixture of death and perverse passion. The melodies of Poe's prose linger, too, with his consummate control of cadence and of open vowel sounds. His is the lingering prose of extremity. The opening tolls like a funereal bell—"Misery is manifold. The wretchedness of earth is multiform"—and in the succeeding pages we learn that the unhappy and unfortunate narrator, Egaeus, will marry his cousin, Berenice, who in the interim becomes emaciated and infirm through the affliction of some unknown disease. They marry, but Egaeus falls victim to an even more insidious disorder. He becomes obsessed with her teeth. In one of Poe's standard motifs, Berenice is buried prematurely. Egaeus wakes from his delirium of sorrow at her apparent death, and then realises that he has torn out the teeth of his bride, while she was yet palpitating in the grave. So the story ends. Poe relied largely upon brevity for effect. All of his endings are abrupt and inconclusive, thus prolonging a mood of uncertainty and even of anxiety. There is always some undertow of meaning, which the reader shares with the author; they are both in the same condition of growing awareness.

It is of course a tale in the Gothic mode, but one that is striated by Poe's own preoccupations. Poe reinvigorated the Gothic tradition of horror and morbid sensationalism by centering it upon the human frame. The image of teeth, perhaps derived from those of his own wasted and emaciated mother, plays some part in his other fictions; the notion of premature burial can be interpreted as a denial of death or as a necrophiliac longing for the moulderings of the grave. Somewhere, among these conflicting interests, Poe's imagination is to be found. In his work death and beauty are powerfully aligned. He was drawn instinctively to the macabre; but for him it was a holy place full of strange scents and echoes. He, of course, might have scorned any such inferences. Poe nicely calculated his effects, and always maintained tight technical control over his narrative. It is significant that he revised continually, making detailed as well as general changes; it may also be worth noting that his handwriting was a model of calligraphy, transcribed on neatly rolled manuscripts, as if all were brought into exquisite order.

There is a point where irony and decay meet, and it is not at all clear whether Poe is laughing or weeping at his own inventions. But there is no necessary disparity between calculation and the expression of the deepest fears and obsessions. He had some intimate connection with his own unconscious anxieties—indeed they guided his life—so he was able instinctively to stir those of his readers. Yet only in disciplined circumstances can those fears be properly formulated. It is the difference between an inchoate wail and a threnody.

. . .

In the spring of 1836 Poe married Virginia in a formal ceremony; presumably he made no reference to a former secret marriage, if such a union ever in fact took place. A witness to the formal marriage, Thomas W. Cleland, declared on oath that the girl was "of the full age of twenty one years." Since Cleland was a pious Presbyterian, he is hardly likely to have sullied the marriage service with an outright fabrication. So Poe lied to him about Virginia's age. Maria Clemm, the mother, must also have lied. Virginia was seven years younger than her stated age, and was in any case regarded as being small for her years. It was a most unlikely union. It was not exactly illegal, but it was unusual.

The newly married Poes seem to have ventured on a short honeymoon, in Petersburg, Virginia, although it is unlikely that their marriage was consummated at the time. He characteristically regarded his relationships with his chosen women as ideal or spiritual in temper. As a result it has been surmised that he was averse to sexual relations of any kind, and even that he was impotent. We can only speculate that physical intimacy with his child bride, if it occurred at all, came at a subsequent date. Some years later, he declared that "I married for another's happiness, when I knew that no possibility of my own existed." This, however, was the self-pity of hindsight.

. . .

In this relatively peaceful period, he grew ever more ambitious for his writing. He dispatched a manuscript of *Tales of the Folio Club* to a New York publisher, but then was advised by a literary friend "to undertake a Tale in a couple of volumes, for that is the magical number." And that is what Poe promptly decided to do. If there was a market, he would address it. He began writing a novel, *The Narrative of Arthur Gordon Pym*, the first instalment of which was published in the *Southern Literary Messenger* for January 1837. Even before it appeared, however, he had been removed from the staff of the periodical. The problem once more arose from his drinking. In September 1836, White had given him notice but was persuaded to reemploy him on certain "conditions"—which conditions, in December, "he has again forfeited." A contemporary in Richmond reported that "when occasionally drinking (the habit was not constant) he was incapacitated for work." He went on "binges," in other words, in the course of which he became incapable. On his own admission he would then be obliged to spend several days in bed, recovering from what was inevitably described as an indisposition.

So Poe "retired" at the beginning of 1837. Three weeks later White wrote to a friend that the *Messenger* "shall outlive all the injury it has sustained from Mr. Poe's management." But it had not sustained any injury at all. Under Poe's direction the magazine attracted more notice, and more praise, than at any time in its subsequent history. Under his management, too, its circulation had risen from 700 to 3,500 subscribers. In addition it had published some of the finest American stories ever written. Poe was already the greatest prose writer in the country. But only a few critics noticed at the time.

Poe remained in Richmond for the rest of January, and wearied White with his importunity. "He is continually after me for money," White wrote. "I am as sick of his writings, as I am of him." And so, at the end of February, Poe and his little household left for New York. He had spent a few months in that city, six years before, but his experience of poverty and misery there had not dissuaded him from returning. It should have done. The opening of "Siope" is suggestive. " 'Listen to *me*,' said the Demon, as he placed his hand upon my head."

CHAPTER SIX

The Editor

The Poes and Maria Clemm went first to a lodging house at Waverly Place, in Greenwich Village, and then later in 1837 moved a few blocks to Carmine Street. A fellow lodger at Waverly Place described Poe as "one of the most courteous, gentlemanly, and intelligent companions I have ever met with"; he added that "I never saw him the least affected with liquor." Yet it was a difficult time, compounded by the fact that in the spring there was a great financial collapse and subsequent panic. In these unpromising circumstances Poe tried to find work as an occasional journalist or reviewer. There is little evidence of any success. Only two of his tales, "Von Jung, the Mystific" and "Siope," were published in this year. The *Messenger* had also given up the serialisation of *The Narrative of Arthur Gordon Pym,* after two instalments. It is not easy to see how Poe and his family survived. It is possible that Mrs. Clemm ran a small boarding house in

Carmine Street—a print shows that it would have been just about large enough to accommodate paying guests— but no other sources of income are known. This was a period, after the "crash," when many people literally starved to death. One of the few extant records concerning Poe reveals that, in the winter of 1837, he called at the Northern Dispensary in Greenwich Village to obtain medicine for a severe cold.

It is not surprising, therefore, that at the beginning of 1838 the little family made its way to Philadelphia. Poe had a habit of moving on, wandering from one city to the next in search of good fortune. He never felt at home anywhere.

Philadelphia was built in gridiron fashion and looked like a chessboard stretched out between the rivers Schuylkill and Delaware; it was one of the oldest, and was still the largest, city in the United States. It was booming. It was expanding. But it was not exhilarating. Poe may have considered himself to be a small piece on the board.

The Poes and Maria Clemm lodged once more in a rooming house. They were poor. They may even have been desperate. The landlord reported that they were "literally suffering for want of food" and were "forced to live on bread and molasses for weeks together." They moved to another lodging house a few weeks later, and then at the end of the year moved again. Poe's employment is not known, except for a reference in a letter to "the miserable life of literary drudgery to which I now, with breaking heart, submit." He had obtained some work as a journalistic hack, writing paragraphs and criticisms to order. He was addressing the new Secretary of the Navy, from whom he begged an appointment as a clerk—*"any thing, by sea or land,"* but nothing was forthcoming.

Yet he was writing. He may have moved to Philadelphia precisely because it was still the publishing centre of the country, with journals such as the *Saturday Evening Post* and the *Gentleman's Magazine*. The city also sustained seven daily morning papers and two daily evening papers. But he was not at first successful in finding employment. Some comfort may have been drawn from the publication by the New York firm of Harpers, that summer, of *The Narrative of Arthur Gordon Pym* in volume form. Yet he never seemed much impressed by his first, and last, novel. Two years after its publication he described it as "a very silly book." That was too harsh a verdict. It was a story that certainly strained credulity, filled with what, on the title page, were called "incredible Adventures and Discoveries," but it was possessed by the strange excitement that issued from Poe's own restless and morbid nature. He had also learned from Daniel Defoe's narratives: he tried to maintain the utmost verisimilitude in order to encompass the wildest improbabilities.

The first chapters concern Arthur Gordon Pym's confinement in a crawl space of a ship, between decks, a subject that elicits all the intensity of Poe's own nature. He thrills to, and yet suffers from, the experience of enclosure. His is the poetry of extremity and of morbidity. In succeding chapters Arthur Gordon Pym is the victim of a callous mutiny, is shipwrecked, suffers from famine, is captured by cannibals and generally reduced to a parodic reenactment of contemporary travellers' adventures. Poe is an artist of the improbable. In one incident Pym attempts to lower himself down a steep precipice, but cannot resist glancing down into the abyss that attracts him; whereupon "my whole soul was pervaded with *a longing to fall*; a desire, a yearning, a passion utterly uncontrollable." This is pure Poe; the unutterable nightmare becomes earnestly wished for. He is the greatest exponent of fantasy fiction in the English language, because he manages to touch upon the most universal or deeply rooted fears. The narrative ends as Pym's boat is drawn towards "the embraces of the cataract," one of the central images of his art. But then there emerges a shrouded being, larger than any human form, whose skin "was of the perfect whiteness of the snow." Poe is drawn to the wildness and mystery of desolation, but he puts no name to it at the end.

The book received what are generally known as "mixed" reviews and was not a financial success. Poe was in such straitened circumstances that he was forced to collude in a slightly shady piece of hack work. He agreed to supply his name, as author, to what was in fact an abbreviated version of a book already in print. *The Conchologist's First Book,* by Edgar A. Poe, was nothing more than a shortened version of Thomas Wyatt's *Manual of Conchology*; Wyatt had hired Poe for the job, because he could not persuade his original publisher to sell an abridgement. It is ironic that it is the only book under Poe's name that ever went into a second edition in his lifetime.

In this year, too, he managed to publish a short story, "Ligeia," in the *American Museum of Literature and the Arts*. It is a tale of metempsychotic horror in which the narrator is devoted to a wife, Ligeia, characterised by "gigantic volition" and "immense" erudition. He is preoccupied by her eyes, dark eyes, *"large eyes"*; in fact Poe claimed that the tale was inspired by a dream in which he saw nothing but female eyes. On Ligeia's death the narrator is besieged by "feelings of utter abandonment." This is the leitmotif, if that is the word, of Poe's art. In this bereft state the narrator marries an Englishwoman for whom he has neither affection nor respect. His loathing materially affects the health of his second wife, and after her death Ligeia herself reemerges within the bandages and draperies of the corpse. So he cries aloud, "These are the full, and the black, and the wild eyes—of my lost love—of the lady—of the LADY LIGEIA." The dead are never wholly dead, and Poe comforts himself with these dreams of the revenant. At a later date he described "Ligeia" as "my *best* tale," its excellence lying in his belief that it most clearly and formally enshrined his purpose. He was the most calculating of authors, never to be confused with his disturbed and even psychotic narrators. Poe the writer strived carefully after the most extreme effects.

. . .

By the end of 1838 he professed himself once more to be desperately poor. Only "by making the most painful sacrifices," by his own account, was he able to pay the rent of his previous lodgings. The Poe household had already moved to a smaller house on Sixteenth Street. Yet, in a life apparently governed by chance or haphazard fate, there was relief at hand. In the late spring of 1839 he proposed himself as an editorial assistant on the staff of the *Gentleman's Magazine*. The editor, William E. Burton, replied that "I wish to form some such engagement as that which you have proposed, and know of no one more likely to suit my views than yourself." In his original letter Poe may have outlined his plans for an "ideal" literary journal that might spread its influence over the entire country. Burton then offered the not princely sum of ten dollars a week, assuring Poe that his duties would only consume two hours a day and leave him time for "any other light avocation" he might wish to pursue; "light avocation" may have referred to Poe's own writing. It was not a promising start. Burton himself was an unusual editor. He was an English comic actor, specialising in the Dickensian roles of Micawber and Captain Cuttle, who had travelled to the United States in order to acquire a reputation as a literary man. Poe was later to describe him as a "buffoon."

Poe began by writing for the *Gentleman's Magazine* (sometimes known as *Burton's Magazine* or, more clumsily, *Burton's Gentleman's Magazine*) an acid review of a Baltimore poet, Rufus Dawes, which Burton then refused to publish on the ground of its severity. Poe wrote to Burton in a state of some dejection, to which the editor replied that "the troubles of the world have given a morbid tone to your feelings which it is your duty to discourage." Nevertheless in the following month, June 1839, Poe formally joined the periodical as assistant editor. Thomas Dunn English, a young poet who used to frequent the offices of the magazine, recalled Poe as always "clad in a plain and rather worn suit of black." He noted, too, that "his eyes at that time were large, bright and piercing, his manner easy and refined, and his tone and conversation winning."

His prose was not so "winning," at least to the contemporary writers whom he despised, and he declared that in his reviews "I intend to put up with nothing that I can *put down.*" He was aware of his own powers. He was aware of his own genius. To see others ranked before him, and praised where he was castigated, aroused all of his combative fury. He could not bear it. So by degrees he acquired a reputation as a querulous and acerbic critic. Undoubtedly this caused him injury among the *literati* of Boston and New York, but his defiance was another sign of his singularity. He knew, too, that he was disliked. "You speak of 'enemies,'" he wrote to one Baltimore journalist, "—could you give me their names?"

But he was also being praised. An article in the *St. Louis Bulletin* remarked that "there are few writers in this country—take Neal, Irving, and Willis away and we would say *none*—who can compete successfully, in many respects, with Poe." Poe was always avid for approval, and liked to advertise the fact that he had been favourably mentioned. So he wrote to the then editor of the *American Museum*, Joseph Evans Snodgrass, asking him to include this notice in any review of the *Gentleman's Magazine*. On a later occasion he told Snodgrass that Washington Irving himself "has addressed me 2 letters, abounding in high passages of compliment." One contemporary noted that "no man living loved the praises of others better than he did; whenever I happened to communicate to him anything touching his abilities as a writer, his bosom would heave like a troubled sea." For all his apparent pride, he had a deep longing to be applauded and recognised. It might have been part of his orphan status in the world.

He had indeed deserved praise. Some of his finest tales were even now being reproduced in the *Gentleman's Magazine*, among them "The Fall of the House of Usher" and "William Wilson." These stories, together with twenty-three others, were published by Lea and Blanchard at the end of 1839 in two volumes entitled *Tales of the Grotesque and Arabesque*. In a short preface to the collection Poe replied to those critics who accused him of "Germanism" or "gloom." "If in many of my productions terror has been the thesis," he wrote, "I maintain that terror is not of Germany but of the soul."

The story of the soul's "terror" that gained most attention, of course, was "The Fall of the House of Usher." It has become one of the classics of the short story or, rather, of the prose poem. It is one of the reasons why Poe was venerated as a master by writers as diverse as

Baudelaire and Maeterlinck. It is a story of unnameable perversities in a house of the mind, a place not of this earth. It is a setting for blood and darkness and mystery.

Roderick Usher is the remnant of a dark and decayed race, living within a mansion imbued with "a pestilent and mystic vapour, dull, sluggish, faintly discernible, and leaden-hued." He lives there, in fear and trembling, together with a sister, the Lady Madeline, who suffers from a "severe and long-continued illness" that no physician can remedy. She expires, even while the narrator of the story remains in the house, and Roderick Usher determines to preserve her corpse for two weeks in one of the vaults within the walls of the ancient mansion. There then follow scenes of turbulence and clangour, in which can be discerned a "most unusual screaming or grating sound." It is the Lady Madeline rising from her interment, emaciated and bloody in her shroud. She has been prematurely buried, but, on seeing her brother, she dies and pulls him down with her on the floor. Thereupon the narrator flees. The house itself is riven and falls into a dark tarn or meer pool beside it, organic and inorganic life dissolving one with another. The morbid and obsessional material here, worked over with infinite finesse, is susceptible to various interpretations, psychic or psychotic. That is why it has endured.

There were many reviewers who derided the material of *Tales* as "slipshod" or "trash," but there were also others who noticed the uniqueness of Poe's prose writing. The commentator in the *American Museum*, for example, believed that the "impress of genius is marked upon them all," and the reviewer of *Alexander's Weekly Messenger* concluded that Poe "has placed himself in the foremost rank of American writers"; the *Saturday Courier* compared him to Coleridge. It is sometimes asserted that Poe was isolated and neglected throughout his writing career. But that is emphatically not the case. He was praised, and celebrated, in many quarters. He was in his own lifetime considered to be one of the most important American writers. That recognition, however, did not mean that he was to be spared a life of poverty and deprivation.

He was given no payment for the newly published *Tales*, for example, and had to be content with a few copies for his own distribution. Nor did the two volumes sell well, and the publishers, two years later, informed Poe that they had not yet "got through" the edition of 750 copies.

Poverty obliged the Poe household once more to move, but in the right direction. They decamped from Sixteenth Street to a three-storey brick house close to the Schuylkill River. It was at the other end of the town, and was a cheaper rent. But Poe felt freer by rivers; he could still swim, and he enjoyed boating expeditions. He often floated on the river, in a small craft, lost within a waking dream. Mrs. Clemm was busy about the housework, and Virginia tended to the garden.

But if this was a refuge from the world, it was not an inviolable one. Thomas Dunn English recalled that "I was passing along the street one night on my way homeward, when I saw someone struggling in a vain attempt to raise himself from the gutter. Supposing the person had tripped and fallen, I bent forward and assisted him to arise. I found it was Poe." English volunteered to assist him home, a wayward progress as a result of Poe's "apparent desire to survey the sidewalk by a series of triangles." Charles Dickens described Philadelphia as "a handsome city, but distractingly regular. After walking about it for an hour or two, I felt that I would have given the world for a crooked street." Poe found his own way of making straight roads crooked.

When eventually Poe and English arrived, Maria Clemm opened the door and cried out, "You make Eddie drunk, and then you bring him home." Poe did not return to the office for two or three days and, when next he saw English, "he was heartily ashamed of the matter." He assured English that it was an "unusual thing" and would never occur again. Several weeks later, however, English learned that Poe had been "found gloriously drunk in the street after nightfall." He did not drink regularly, in other words, but, when he did, he could not stop. The red mist fell upon him. There are reports, too, that he was getting into "bad company." These were no doubt the printers and hack journalists and poetasters who frequented the offices of the local journals. Poe's employer, William Burton, was becoming steadily disenchanted with his assistant editor, and complained to anyone who would listen that Poe had been getting drunk when he should have been working.

Burton was in any case losing interest in the magazine.

He was engaged in the construction in Philadelphia of a grandly named National Theatre, and in May 1840 he advertised the *Gentleman's Magazine* for sale. Poe, learning of his intentions, decided to announce the imminent arrival of his own journal under his own editorship.

The separation of owner and assistant editor was inevitable. At the end of the month Poe was dismissed from the *Gentleman's Magazine*; or, rather, he claimed that he had retired "in uncontrollable disgust" at Burton's "chicanery, arrogance, ignorance and brutality." He had been writing a serial of adventure for the magazine, "The Journal of Julius Rodman," but he broke it off practically in midsentence. It remained unfinished. In the pages of the *Gentleman's Magazine* itself Burton retaliated by printing an apologetic letter to a subscriber whose name had been "erased from our list by the person whose 'infirmities' have caused us much annoyance." In turn Poe described Burton as a "felon" as well as a "buffoon." A brief partnership had once more ended in disaster.

Poe was serious, however, about the alternative journal under his own editorship. He had been contemplating the idea for some time, and in June he composed a prospectus for what he entitled the *Penn Magazine*; the name was a pun on "pen" and the abbreviation of Pennsylvania. He anticipated the "versatility, originality and pungency" of its contributions; he declared that it would soon become known as a periodical "where may be found, at all times, and upon all subjects, an honest and a fearless opinion"; it would belong "to the loftiest regions of literature." And it would cost five dollars per annum. He was convinced that it would make his fortune, and at one stroke remove him from the importunities of any employer. He was sure of his ability to reshape or to reformulate American letters.

Almost at once he began to write to editors, publishers, and journalists in the hope of acquiring a subscription list. He wanted to gather five hundred names by the beginning of December, thus putting his enterprise on a secure foundation. He even wrote to other members of the Poe family in search of financial contributions. He was also gathering material for the first number, which he confidently predicted would be ready by the beginning of 1841. Yet his ambitions, at this stage, outran his achievement. He found the preliminary work "difficult and most arduous," and towards the end of the year he contracted some unspecified ailment that consigned him to bed for a month. This "severe illness," as he called it, effectively delayed his plans for publication. He altered the date of the first issue from January to March 1841. But then in February there was another financial crash or panic in which the major banks in Philadelphia, and the South, were forced to close their doors. It was the worst possible moment for Poe's venture. It collapsed. It was a part of the ill fortune that followed him everywhere.

So how was he now to live? In a life of unrest and poverty he depended upon the merest chance to rescue his family from devastation. That chance returned in the shape of the erstwhile *Gentleman's Magazine*. William Burton had sold the journal to a young lawyer from

Philadelphia, George Rex Graham. Graham promptly changed the title to *Graham's Lady's and Gentleman's Magazine*, but, with little journalistic or literary experience, he needed someone to assist him. Burton himself might have recommended the assistant editor whom he had fired eight months previously. Animosities, in this world, rarely endured for long. And so, in the spring of 1841, Graham offered Poe a salary of eight hundred dollars a year as editor of the book reviews. Poe accepted immediately—with "great pleasure," as he put it—and once more set to work on another's behalf.

A somewhat sentimental and saccharine affair, with well-meaning verses and tame "thrillers" and illustrations of pets and children, it was not the ideal literary journal of his prospectus. Yet Poe dismissed any misgivings he might have felt, and over the next two years published in its pages some nine new stories, fifty-one reviews, and fifteen essays. Here appeared, for example, "The Murders in the Rue Morgue" and "A Descent into the Maelstrom."

He considered it a temporary appointment, however, designed to shield him from immediate hardship. Just five months after accepting the post he was actively seeking a clerkship in a political office in Washington. The intermediary was Frederick W. Thomas, whom he had met a year before at a convention in Philadelphia. Thomas was a novelist and journalist who had known Poe's brother, Henry; he also drank a great deal, and had aspirations to literary fame. So a friendship was formed. Thomas was in fact one of the few close friends Poe ever made. Thomas had acquired a sinecure in Washington, sifting through applications to the department of the Treasury, and he held out to Poe the prospect of similar employment. Poe wrote back enthusiastically. He was "really serious about the office." He confided to Thomas that "notwithstanding Graham's unceasing civility, and real kindness, I feel more & more disgusted with my situation." He was a hired hand on a mediocre publication.

Yet he was earning the largest income he had so far enjoyed. He told one acquaintance that "I am temperate even to rigor," and for the first time in his adult life he was free of debt. He purchased some unaccustomed luxuries, including a four-poster bed, a porcelain dinner service, and, for Virginia, a piano and a harp. He attended literary dinners, mingling with other authors and other publishers, and was also a frequent visitor at Graham's own table. It is reported that Maria Clemm would wait in Graham's kitchen, with the express purpose of keeping Poe from excessive drinking and of accompanying him home.

The hope of a Washington post, like all of Poe's aspirations, came to nothing. But, in the autumn of 1841, he reached an agreement with Graham to stay at his editorial post through the following year. There is every reason why Graham would wish him to continue. The circulation of the periodical had climbed from five thousand to twenty-five thousand, and that rise had more than a little to do with the publication of Poe's tales and reviews. Through his agency *Graham's Magazine*, as it was universally called, would soon become the largest selling monthly magazine in America.

Poe once described himself as "essentially a Magazinist," and, in certain respects, he did have the sensibility of a journalist. He had an eye for effect, a predilection for novelty, an interest in contemporary crazes such as phrenology and ballooning, and a shrewd notion of the public taste for "sensation." He wrote to one correspondent that the whole tendency of the age was towards magazine literature—"to the curt, the terse, the well timed, and the readily diffused, in preference to the old forms of the verbose and ponderous . . ." It might almost be a definition of his fiction. He was always in the marketplace.

After Poe's death, Graham wrote a tribute to him in which he described him as "punctual and unwearied in his industry—*and the soul of honor*, in all his transactions . . . He kept his accounts, small as they were, with the accuracy of a banker." He also extolled him as a "polished gentleman" and a "devoted husband," even in "his high-hearted struggle with adverse fate." Graham left a small detail that helps to explain the nature of the Poe household: "What he received from me in regular monthly instalments, went directly into the hands of his mother-in-law . . ."

Poe believed now that he had written enough new tales, in *Graham's Magazine* and elsewhere, to offer an expanded volume of them to Lea and Blanchard. He wished it to be called *Phantasy Pieces* and would include the tales already published by that firm under the title of *Tales of the*

Grotesque and Arabesque, as well as eight more recently written tales. Lea and Blanchard refused the offer, on the grounds that they still had unsold stock of the previous publication.

Among the rejected tales was "The Murders in the Rue Morgue," which in later years was hailed as the harbinger of the modern detective story. It was fashioned around the character of C. Auguste Dupin, the French detective who resolves the most grotesque or ambiguous crimes with the keen logic of calculation. Dupin might be a version of his author. Poe prided himself on his intimacy with the secrets of cryptography, and successfully resolved the most apparently insoluble or enigmatic codes. He even started a series of papers in *Graham's Magazine* in which he challenged all exponents of "secret messages." He loved the idea of unravelling secret writings, of saying the unsayable. Could the idea of the secret also be related to the mystery of his father's disappearance and of his mother's supposed disgrace? He boasted to a friend that "nothing intelligible can be written which, with time, I cannot decipher." And so it proved.

He said that "the *highest* order of the imaginative intellect is always pre-eminently mathematical" and that genius itself consisted of "method." But the assumption of analysis and calculation was in part artificial: he confessed that the power of his studies lay in their "*air* of method."

Poe evinced another form of calculation, too. He was often very sly, or subtle, in his dealing with other people. He was a great calculator in human relationships, ever watchful of himself and of others. He strove after certain effects with the brilliant ease of a born manipulator. In one letter he confessed that "the peevishness was all 'put on' as a part of my argument—of my plan:—so was the 'indignation' with which I wound up." Yet there is something almost childlike about this trait in his character. He suffered agonies after any drinking bout, in part because he hated the sensation of losing all sense of calculation.

Many of his most successful stories are, therefore, "tales of ratiocination." The word "detective" was not coined until 1843. Dupin is, perhaps, the first. As such he is the forerunner of such diverse "ratiocinators" as Sherlock Holmes and Father Brown. As Arthur Conan Doyle put it, Poe "was father of the detective tale, and covered its limits so completely I fail to see how his followers can find ground to call their own." Dupin is a bachelor, with an amanuensis who records the details of his investigation; he has only a provisional contact with the police, who come to solicit his help with the crimes they cannot solve. In "The Murders in the Rue Morgue," these concern the gruesome murders of a mother and young daughter. But Dupin subjects these events to impersonal and objective analysis. He is the Newton of the criminal world. Through a process of deduction and elimination Dupin comes to the conclusion that the perpetrator was not a human being at all. So he sets a trap. Poe described the story as "something in a new key."

One of the other stories of this period, "Eleanora," has a curious resonance in Poe's life. The narrator, Pyrros, has married his fifteen-year-old cousin. "We lived all alone, knowing nothing of the world without the valley—I, and my cousin, and her mother." This is an image of Poe's own existence, of course, but in his imagination events take a fatal turn. The young bride dies of consumption. Before her death she wrings a promise from Pyrros that he will never love another woman. But, in that, he proves false to her. The rest of the story is not important, with its maladroit "happy ending," but there was another and more immediate parallel. A few months after this story was composed, Virginia herself succumbed to the first stages of consumption.

CHAPTER SEVEN

The Man
Who Never Smiled

In the middle of January 1842, Virginia Poe had been singing at the piano, one of her favourite pastimes, when she stopped suddenly; she began coughing up blood. Poe considered it to be the rupture of a blood vessel, but the effusion is more likely to have been from her weakened lungs.

After the irruption she required the utmost attention, but circumstances were far from ideal for the care of an invalid. One neighbour reported that she was obliged to lie in a narrow bed, in a tiny bedroom with a ceiling so low that her head almost touched it; here she suffered, hardly able to breathe. But no one dared to mention the cramped surroundings to Poe, who had become "oversensitive and irritable"; "quick as steel and flint" said one who knew him in those days. Graham recalled that he would hover about his wife's bed, alert to every tremor and cough with "a shudder, a heart-chill that was visible." And he would not allow a word about the danger of her dying—"the mention of it drove him wild."

Yet he still wrote about death endlessly. In "Life in Death," a painter wishes to portray his young bride; but, in the turret room which is his studio, she pines and sickens to death. By painting her, he kills her. In the same year Poe wrote "The Masque of the Red Death," a story of death and pestilence in which "blood was its Avatar and its seal—the redness and the horror of blood." He wrote "The Mystery of Marie Roget," in which a young girl is murdered by person or persons unknown. He wrote "The Tell-Tale Heart," a story of intolerable intensity told by a maniac; this close and almost suffocating narrative concludes with a cry of terror, "here, here! it is the beating of his hideous heart!" In this same year, too, he wrote "Lenore," an encomium upon a young woman and "A dirge for her the doubly dead in that she died so young."

He wandered about the streets for hours, in despair, until Mrs. Clemm became so alarmed by his absence that she would leave the house in search of him. At this time, too, he began once more to drink. In periods of the utmost distress and anxiety, it was for him the natural course. No force on earth could have prevented him. Of Virginia he wrote that "at each accession of the disorder I loved her more dearly and clung to her life with more desperate pertinacity." But then "I became insane, with long intervals of horrible sanity. During these fits of absolute unconsciousness, I drank—God only knows how often or how much." He related the drink to the insanity, but it is more likely that the temporary insanity emerged from the drink. He had an unusually nervous constitution, and any assault upon it had dangerous consequences.

In the spring of 1842 he resigned from *Graham's*, on the apparent grounds of his "disgust with the namby-pamby character of the Magazine . . . I allude to the contemptible pictures, fashion-plates, music and love tales." But the real reasons lie deeper. He had once more become "irregular" in his editorial habits. He and a colleague had quarrelled violently, no doubt when Poe was in drink. Then, after one forced absence of some days, he returned to the office only to find someone else occupying his chair. He had no choice but to leave. He would not willingly have forfeited an annual income of eight hundred dollars.

He told one acquaintance in a letter that in any case "the state of my mind" had forced him to abandon "all mental exertion." His wife's illness, his own ill health and poverty "have nearly driven me to distraction. My only hope of relief is the 'Bankrupt Act' . . . but the struggle to keep up has, at length, entirely ruined me." In the last sentences of this letter he wrote that "Mrs. Poe is again dangerously ill with haemorrhage from the lungs. It is folly to hope." It seemed that the world was closing in around him; nothing but darkness lay ahead of him. It was in this period that he wrote "The Pit and the Pendulum." Yet, against all the odds, he did hope. He hoped to obtain a clerkship in the Customs House at Philadelphia, again through the agency of Thomas. He hoped to revive the plans for his own journal, the *Penn Magazine*.

There was one curious incident, however, in the early summer of 1842 that throws a different light upon his high expectations. Poe had decided to travel to New York in order to find journalistic work, and to contact publishers likely to look favourably upon a new collection of his stories. But he drank himself into a state of inanition. He decided, in that condition, to call upon the old friend or "sweetheart" he had known in Baltimore eleven years before; Mary Devereaux, or "Baltimore Mary" as he called her in memory of happier times, had now become Mrs. Jennings. He had forgotten where she lived in Jersey City, and spent many hours crossing and recrossing the Hudson River on the ferry, accosting strangers and asking for her address. Eventually, by some miracle, he obtained it. He was fleeing from a sick wife to a young woman, one to whom he may once have been unofficially engaged. He was seeking some comfort, some recompense, in the memory of an earlier affection.

His unexpected arrival caused something of a commotion, and Mary recalled that "we saw he was on one of his sprees, and he had been away from home for several days." He was, in other words, disoriented and dirty and dishevelled. He reproached his hostess for her marriage, saying that in truth she loved him only. This is an odd remark, from a man whose own wife was fatally ill. He asked Mary to sing and play the piano, meanwhile becoming "excited in conversation." Poe then minced up some radishes with such fury that pieces of them flew about the room. He drank a cup of tea, and departed.

Several days later Maria Clemm arrived at the same house, desperately looking for "Eddie dear." According to Mary, "a search was made, and he was finally found in the woods on the outskirts of Jersey City, wandering about like a crazy man." The story may have been elaborated, but the gist seems authentic enough. No one could have made up the detail about the radishes.

. . .

He visited New York on another occasion, when again he became incapacitated by drink. He wrote an apologetic letter to a friend there, asking him to be "kind enough to put the best possible interpretation upon my behaviour while in N-York? You must have conceived a *queer* idea of me—but the simple truth is that Wallace [a poet] would insist upon the *juleps*, and I knew not what I was either doing or saying." It was his habit to blame others for the extent of his drinking. It was, perhaps, the only way he could make sense of it.

By the following year the news of his drinking had become part of the gossip of Philadelphia. An acquaintance of his from Baltimore days, Lambert Wilmer, told a mutual friend that "he is going headlong to destruction, moral, physical and intellectual." Poe was in such straitened circumstances that he was offering his latest tale, "The Mystery of Marie Roget," at a low price to both the Boston *Notion* and the *Baltimore Saturday Visiter*. The loss of any regular income had consigned the Poe household to a state of real distress. They moved to a smaller house on the outskirts of Philadelphia, where Frederick Thomas visited them in the autumn of 1842. He noticed that "everything about the place wore an air of pecuniary want" and that "there was delay and evident difficulty in procuring the meal." Maria Clemm and Virginia expressed the wish to Thomas that "Eddie" might obtain some kind of steady work, but "I was not long in observing with deep regret that he had fallen again into habits of intemperance." They made an arrangement to meet the following day, but Poe did not keep the appointment; he wrote later to say that he had fallen ill. It was his usual excuse.

He was still actively pursuing the position of clerk in the Customs House at Philadelphia. He believed the post to be assured but, as so often in his life, his hopes were raised "only to be dashed to the ground." That was the phrase he used in a letter to Thomas, in which he detailed the insolence and hauteur of the petty official in whom he had placed his trust. It was always his fate to be thwarted. It cannot be said, however, that he had any interest in any form of government administration. He was wholly out of sympathy with American politics and questioned once "Is it or is it not a fact that the air of a Democracy agrees better with mere Talent than with Genius?" He was a proponent of slavery, and a believer in what he called "caste." He had no faith in progress, or in democracy, and so was in a real sense divorced from the life of America—or at least of that spirit embodied by the Northern states.

Yet he had been hoping for the appointment, too, as a means of continuing his scheme for a literary journal under his direction. He had been confidently planning for the publication of the first number at the beginning of 1843; but in this, as in so many of the affairs of his life, he was disappointed. Even as he was dogged with ill luck, however, someone else turned up to rescue him. He became acquainted with the editor of the Philadelphia *Saturday Museum*, Thomas C. Clarke, who was the perfect partner in the enterprise. Poe had decided to rename the prospective journal, changing it from the *Penn* to the *Stylus*. Clarke had agreed to finance the venture, while allowing Poe a half-interest in it. At last Poe had achieved "the great object—a partner possessing ample capital, and, at the same time, so little self-esteem, as to allow me entire control of the editorial conduct." Was it too good to be true?

Armed with a signed agreement, Poe distributed a new prospectus on the merits of a magazine that would be established upon "the purest rules of Art" and would "far surpass all American journals of its kind." He wished it to be "the great literary journal of the future," as he told one acquaintance. He also embarked upon a course of self-advertisement by arranging for a sketch of his life to be printed in the *Saturday Museum* itself. It was little more than a "puff," but he believed that it would materially assist the fortunes of the *Stylus*. He provided the material himself, of course, but it did not err on the side of veracity. It was revealed that Poe had travelled to Greece and to Russia, and that he had somehow returned from Europe on the night of Frances Allan's funeral. He was described as "somewhat slender, about five feet, eight inches in height, and well proportioned; his complexion is rather fair, his eyes are grey and restless, exhibiting a marked nervousness; while the mouth indicates great decision of character . . ."

The *Spirit of the Times*, another Philadelphian journal, noticed the biographical sketch and applauded Poe as one "of the most powerful, chaste and erudite writers of the day." The *Museum* in turn announced that Poe was to become its associate editor and that his fame "shall be placed beyond the reach of conjecture." It was a joint enterprise in log-rolling that no doubt appealed to Poe's vanity. In fact he never did join the staff of the *Museum*. It was another of the convenient fictions by which he chose to live.

His hopes for the *Stylus*, however, sent him to Washington in search of subscribers. He was also planning to renew his endless quest for a clerkship, and even entertained a fantasy of meeting President Tyler himself in order to plead for his cause. It was not, however, an auspicious journey. Almost as soon as he had taken a room at Fuller's City Hotel, he began to drink. On the first evening, according to an acquaintance, he was "over-persuaded to take some Port wine" and became "somewhat excited." Two days later he met a fellow journalist on the street who reported him to be "seedy in appearance and woebegone." He begged fifty cents, complaining that "he had not had a mouthful of food since the day previous." On the following day Poe himself wrote to his new partner, Thomas Clarke, with the news that "I believe that I am making a *sensation* which will tend to the benefit of the Magazine."

This was sheer self-delusion on his part, although he was perhaps creating a "sensation" in quite a different sense. He was once more drinking to excess. The editor of the Washington *Index*, Jesse Dow, had known Poe four years before. They had worked together on *Burton's* magazine in Philadelphia. Now he had the unenviable job of escorting Poe through the city. Dow tried to escape the responsibility by writing a solemn letter to Clarke, telling him that "I think it advisable for you to come on and see him safely back to his home." Dow added that "Mrs. Poe is in a bad state of health, and I charge you, as you have a soul to be saved, to say not one word to her about him until he arrives with you." Three days later Poe boarded the train from Washington to Philadelphia, where he found Maria Clemm anxiously waiting for him at the station. That evening he visited Clarke, no doubt in order to dispel any unfortunate impressions Clarke might have derived from Dow's letter. "He received me, therefore, very cordially & made light of the matter," he wrote to Thomas and Dow jointly. "I told him what had been agreed upon—that I was a little sick & that Dow, knowing I had been, in times past, given to spreeing upon an extensive scale, had become unduly alarmed etcetera . . ." So he had agreed upon a story with his intimates to cover his excesses.

But there is no doubt that he was once again mortified by his behaviour under the influence of drink. To Dow he wrote "thank you a thousand times for your kindness & great forbearance, & don't say a word about the cloak turned inside out, or other peccadilloes of that nature. Also, express to your wife my deep regret for the vexation I must have occasioned her." Then he asked Thomas to send his compliments "to the Don, whose mustachios I do admire after all . . . express my regret to Mr. Fuller for making such a fool of myself in his house . . ." So he had paraded through the streets wearing his cloak inside out, and had made fun of a Spaniard's moustache. He had also behaved badly in someone's house. These are not hanging offences, and may have been a source of amusement to those around him. But he had a deep sense of pride, as well as an instinctive sense of formality and control. When these were abrogated and injured, he fell into sickness and grief. His illnesses were caused not by physical over-indulgence but by guilty self-laceration.

The result of the Washington debacle was, of course, that he did not gain an interview with President Tyler or retain any hope of obtaining the clerkship. It is also doubt-ful whether he enlisted many subscribers for the new peri-odical. Or, if he had, that he would be able to remember them. "Did you say Dow," he wrote to his friend in a post-script, "that Commodore Elliot had desired me to put down his name? Is it so or did I dream it?" Poe was com-pletely unsuited to arranging the economic management, or financial future, of any enterprise.

. . .

Soon after his return from Washington, the Poe household decamped once again. The pressure of debt kept them moving on. They had now arrived in a suburb of Philadelphia, in the district known as Spring Garden, and were lodged in a wooden plank-built "lean-to" of three rooms. This was the account of their dwelling given by a neighbour, Captain Wayne Reid, who became acquainted with them. Reid characterised Maria Clemm as "a woman of middle age, and almost masculine aspect." It seemed astonishing to him that she should be the mother of "a lady angelically beautiful in person and not less beautiful in spirit."

Reid also left a description of Maria Clemm's familial role. "She was the ever vigilant guardian of the home," he wrote, "watching it against the silent but continuous sap of necessity . . . She was the sole servant, keeping everything clean; the sole messenger, doing the errands, making the pilgrimages between the poet and his publishers . . . And she was also the messenger to the market; from it bringing back not 'the delicacies of the season,' but only such commodities as were called for by the dire exigencies of hunger."

Yet despite its privations, and Virginia's illness, the family appeared to others to be relatively contented. Another neighbour recalled that in the mornings "Mrs. Clemm and her daughter would be generally watering the flowers . . . They seemed always cheerful and happy, and I could hear Mrs. Poe's laugh before I turned the corner. Mrs. Clemm was always busy. I have seen her of mornings clearing the front yard, washing the windows and the stoop, and even white-washing the palings." Everyone remarked upon the neatness, and cleanliness, of the various Poe abodes. Maria Clemm also rented out the front room of the Spring Garden house to lodgers. This was one way of alleviating their endless poverty.

And what of Poe himself? Another neighbour, Lydia Hart Garrigues, a young girl who lived on the same street, recalled that he "wore a Spanish cloak." She noted that "I was always impressed with the grave and thoughtful aspect of his face . . . He, his wife and Mrs. Clemm kept to themselves. They had the reputation of being very reserved—we thought because of their poverty and his great want of success." Miss Garrigues added that "it was not until after 'The Raven' was published . . . that we knew him as a literary figure." It might have interested her to know that, in fact, Poe had already begun the writing of that famous poem while residing in Spring Garden. It had a long gestation, and by Poe's account it was accompanied by an amount of calculation and technical experiment that would have wearied Milton and Sophocles combined. He wanted the bird to be an owl, but then changed his mind. So here, in Philadelphia, was hatched the raven.

There also emerged a prize-winning short story. Poe's tale of adventure and detection, "The Gold Bug," won a hundred dollar prize from the *Dollar Newspaper*. It is a story concerning the discovery of hidden treasure, set in the neighbourhood of Sullivan's Island, where Poe had been stationed as a private soldier fifteen years before. The subtropical beaches, with their "dense undergrowth of the sweet myrtle . . . burthening the air with its fragrance," provide the atmosphere for a tale of invisible ink and cryptography, enigmatic codes and secret instructions. "The Gold Bug" may not hold sufficient interest for a contemporary audience, but Poe's first readers deemed it "a production of superior merit" in which all the pleasures of verisimilitude were maintained within the context of a quest for fabled gold. Poe could quite rightly be construed as a second Defoe, whose *Robinson Crusoe* he had praised very highly for its constant pursuit of veracity and probability. The *Saturday Museum*, Poe's usual champion, described the story as "the most remarkable piece of American fiction that has been published within the last fifteen years." The edition of the *Dollar Newspaper* containing the first part was sold out.

There was one reader, however, who was not so impressed by what he called "unmitigated trash" and a piece of "humbug"—the "humbug" consisting of that very air of veracity cast over a series of remarkable events. The author of this attack, F.H. Duffee, then suggested that Poe had actually been paid only ten or fifteen dollars rather than the supposed full prize. So Poe sued him for libel, claiming that his "character for integrity" had been injured. He hired a lawyer, and signed an affidavit in the District Court. There were many who made fun of Poe's sudden sensitivity, noting that he had in the past published "severe and scorching criticisms" of his own. But the action came to nothing. A week after Poe's appearance in court, he and Duffee met, resolved their differences, and signed an agreement.

On hearing the news of the prize from the *Dollar Newspaper*, Poe's cousin, William Poe, sent him a congratulatory letter in which he hoped that the money would help to relieve "the sickness & despondency you were suffering when you last wrote." So Poe had been announcing his feelings even to members of his own family. William Poe also wished to caution his cousin against that "which has been a great enemy to our family." The enemy was, of course, a "too free use of the Bottle." The Bottle was the demon of the Poes. In the summer of 1843 Poe was satirised in print as a drunkard. He was lampooned in a novel by Thomas Dunn English, *The Drunkard's Doom*, in which he was characterised as "the very incarnation of treachery and falsehood." It was the first, but by no means the last, occasion that Poe entered a work of fiction.

His appearance was also the object of much comment and speculation. He was five feet eight inches in height, and held himself erect with an almost military bearing; he invariably wore black, with a black frockcoat and black cravat as if he were in perpetual mourning. He was of slender, or slight, build; he had dark brown hair, slightly curled, and grey eyes that were variously described as "restless" or as "large and liquid." His broad forehead was noticeable, emphasising what was known in the language of phrenology (in which he believed) as the "bump of ideality." His mouth was thin, and seemed to others to be expressive of scorn or discontent; sometimes it seemed even to form a sneer. His complexion was pale, his features very fine. In 1845 he grew a moustache, which was long rather than heavy. His manner was "nervous and emphatic," his visage prone to what one contemporary called the "*nervousness* of expression so peculiar to Poe." That expression was generally deemed to be sad or melancholy or sombre or grave or dreamy. A judicious mixture of these will give an approximate clue to his general appearance. But there was one other detail. In the extant photographs there was some contrast or disjunction between the right and left sides of the face, with slight but noticeable differences in the eye and mouth, brow and chin. One side was weaker than the other.

. . .

In the autumn of 1843 Poe told a fellow writer in Philadelphia that "his wife and Mrs. Clemm were starving." So fifteen dollars were promptly raised from journalists and others; an hour after the money had been given to Poe, "he was found in a state of intoxication in Decatur Street." This was the street that harboured the Decatur Coffee House, which advertised its "Mint Juleps, Cobblers, Egg Noggs etcetera."

He had in the meantime been disappointed with the sales of a new edition of his tales. Graham's brother had agreed to publish a "Uniform Serial Edition of the Prose Romances of Edgar A. Poe." It was to comprise a series of cheaply produced pamphlets, at a price of twelve-and-a-half cents, but the first of them included only "The Murders in the Rue Morgue" and "The Man that Was Used Up." It was noticed by two or three local journals, but the fact that no further pamphlets were issued is proof enough that the enterprise was not a success. There were several tales, now written but still not published—among them "The Premature Burial." "The Purloined Letter," and "Thou Art the Man." It can be said with some certainty that Poe's true genius was not recognised until after his death.

So with his authorial career in abeyance, his journalistic career in the doldrums, and his plans for the *Stylus* indefinitely postponed, he embarked upon a course of lectures. On 21 November 1843 he addressed an audience in Philadelphia on "American Poetry"; according to the *United States Gazette* "hundreds . . . were unable to gain admission" to the Julianna Street Church where the lecture was held. It was successful enough, in any case, for him to repeat the experience in the Temperance Hall in Wilmington, at Newark Academy in Delaware, at the Mechanics Institute in Reading, and at the Lecture Room of the Philadelphia Museum. He then went on to the Odd Fellows' Hall in Baltimore.

He was trenchant. He denounced the system of "puffery" then in vogue with the American press, and exposed the fraudulence of authors reviewing their own books or praising those of their friends. These were not faults from which Poe himself was free. He then went on to examine the merits of the American poets, concentrating largely upon the "collections," or anthologies, which were then highly popular. He singled out Rufus Griswold's

Poets and Poetry of America, which he praised as the "best" of the current compilations, but then condemned Griswold, the editor, for "a miserable want of judgement—the worst specimens being chosen instead of the best—and an extravagant amount of space being allotted to personal friends . . ."

Poe had met Griswold two years before, and they had circled each other in mutual suspicion masked by professed admiration. Griswold had succeeded Poe at *Graham's Magazine*, where he gained a reputation for literary chicanery. But the publication of his anthology in 1842 brought him a measure of success. Poe was ambivalent, describing it as "a most outrageous humbug" to a private correspondent while lauding it in print as "the most important addition which our literature has for many years received." The protestation was not enough. When a wholly and sarcastically negative review of Griswold's anthology appeared in the *Saturday Museum*, Griswold assumed (wrongly, as it happened) that Poe had composed it. Then there came Poe's animadversions upon the book in his series of lectures. But Griswold eventually had his revenge. After Poe's death he would be responsible for the most lethal character assassination in the history of American literature.

. . .

In April 1844 the Poe household was on the move again, its destination being once more New York. The fact that his previous experiences there had been almost uniformly unhappy did not deter him. What could be worse than poverty in Philadelphia?

Poe and Virginia went on ahead, travelling by train and steamboat, and the morning after their arrival Poe sent a long letter to Maria Clemm. "When we got to the wharf," he reported, "it was raining hard. I left her on board the boat, after putting the trunks in the Ladies' Cabin, and set off to buy an umbrella and bought one for 62 cents." He originally wrote "56," and then changed it to "62." The extra expense of six cents was important for one such as Maria Clemm.

Poe went up Greenwich Street, and soon found a boarding house that surpassed his expectations. "Last night, for supper, we had the nicest tea you ever drank . . ." Then he went on to expatiate upon the meats and cheeses and breads placed on the table before them. Virginia, or "Sis," "has coughed hardly any and had no night sweat. She is now busy mending my pants which I tore against a nail." For Poe, this letter is remarkably unguarded. He added in a matter of fact manner that he was going out to borrow money—a sign of how common an occupation that had become for him—and noted that "I feel in excellent spirits & haven't drank a drop—so that I hope so to get out of trouble." This is the clearest sign that Poe was an habitual drinker, and that Maria Clemm knew it. There was no need for obfuscation or excuse. If he stayed clear of drink, then he might also stay out of "trouble"—the trouble being general wretchedness, and an inability to work.

This time, he stayed true to his word. Within a week of his arrival he had sold a story of sensation to the *New York Sun*. On April 13 that newspaper carried the headline, ASTOUNDING INTELLIGENCE BY PRIVATE EXPRESS FROM CHARLESTON VIA NORFOLK! THE ATLANTIC OCEAN CROSSED IN THREE DAYS!! ARRIVAL AT SULLIVAN'S ISLAND OF A STEERING BALLOON INVENTED BY MR. MONCK MASON!! It was one of Poe's most successful "spoofs" or "hoaxes," a game in which he delighted. It suited his propensity both for calculation and for comedy. The newspaper published an extra edition that afternoon, and it was rapidly sold out. Poe wrote that "I never witnessed more intense excitement to get possession of a newspaper." The newsboys were charging outrageous prices, and Poe himself could not get hold of a copy all that day. Two days later, after a chorus of disbelief and disapproval, the *Sun* retracted its "scoop." But the power of Poe's pen had been proved beyond doubt.

"The Balloon Hoax" is one of his most celebrated stories, not least because it opened the path for later writers of science fantasy including Jules Verne and H.G. Wells. It has even been suggested that Poe is the forerunner of nineteenth- and twentieth-century science fiction. If that accolade is placed beside his claim to be the originator of the detective story, then Poe left a distinguished legacy. "The Balloon Hoax" purports to be the journal of

Mr. Monck Mason, a real aeronaut who had already flown by balloon from Vauxhall Gardens to Weilberg in Germany. So Poe adopts his name and contrives a fantastic adventure for him; Mason performs what was then considered an impossible feat and, by ingenious arrangement of valves and air, manages to steer his balloon across the Atlantic. Poe was a century ahead of the actual achievement, but there is nothing in his account that strains credulity. It is a thoroughly practical enterprise, narrated in a direct and unmediated style of journalistic reportage. Poe had perpetrated a similar hoax some nine years before in "Hans Phaall—A Tale," in which a journey by balloon to the moon is outlined in some detail; he had written this at the age of twenty-six. He always enjoyed these fantasies. They were a form of satire, directed against the "crazes" of the moment. But they were also a form of ratiocination, a challenge to create a suitable and perfectly plausible set of circumstances by which the impossible could be conveyed with the utmost verisimilitude.

. . .

In the spring of 1844 Maria Clemm, together with the black cat Catterina, joined her daughter in Greenwich Street, while Poe stayed temporarily in bachelor's quarters. But they were all soon on the move again. In early June the household took lodgings in a farmhouse some five miles outside New York, in a rural spot now to be identified as the corner of Eighty-fourth Street and Broadway. Here, in the words of a contemporary, was "a wilderness of rocks, bushes, and thistles with here and there a farm house." But the front windows looked down into the valley of the Hudson, and took in the sweep of the river. He described the place later as "a perfect heaven," and in these more tranquil surroundings it was to be hoped that his own nervous terrors would abate and that Virginia's malady might improve. The son of the landlord, Tom Brennan, later recalled that Poe would take walks into the country or beside the nearby river; then, in the afternoon, he would return and "work unceasingly with pen and paper until the evening shadows." Tom's sister, Martha Brennan, recalled the weakness of Virginia, who was sometimes so frail that Poe would have to carry her into dinner. There is one other significant point. The landlady, Mrs. Brennan, was an uncompromising supporter of the temperance movement. Perhaps Poe refrained from drinking during his stay in her farmhouse.

Dollars were, as usual, in short supply. He managed to pay Mrs. Brennan, but sometimes he did not have the cents to claim the letters waiting for him at the local post office. In this period the recipient, not the sender, paid for the mail. He liked life in the country so much, however, that he did not wish to return to the city to look for work. But, as usual, Maria Clemm took matters into her own hands. At the end of September she made one of her infrequent visits to the city and called upon Nathaniel P. Willis, the editor of a newly launched daily newspaper, the *Evening Mirror*, asking or rather begging for work to be given to her son-in-law. Willis was already a well-known magazine journalist, who supplied an endless stream of witty and fanciful pieces for an increasingly receptive public; but he sensed Poe's talent, and defended his reputation before and after Poe's death. According to Willis, Maria Clemm "excused her errand by mentioning that Poe was ill, that her daughter was a confirmed invalid, and that their circumstances were such as compelled her taking it upon herself."

Poe was thereupon enrolled as a "mechanical paragraphist," no very exalted position in a profession where he had already been an acting editor. His job consisted principally in condensing items from other papers, culling material from the French press that might be suitable for an American audience, and in general providing amusing "copy." His post at the *Mirror* entailed a five-mile walk each way from the farmhouse. The omnibus fare was a shilling, a sum that Poe could scarcely have afforded. So in the winter of 1844 the Poe family moved back into the city, and took rented apartments once more in Greenwich Street. He was now close to his work.

Willis recalled to a colleague "how absolutely and how good-humouredly ready he was for any suggestion, how punctually and industriously reliable . . . how cheerful and present-minded in his work when he might excusably have been so listless and abstracted." This is an account of Poe to be placed beside the more lurid and dramatic notices of his intoxication. In the right circumstances, even in the face of his young wife's lingering disease, he was courteous and industrious. He was dogged by poverty, and

Eliza Poe—Poe's mother, an actress who died young, leaving him an orphan.

Fanny Allan—Poe's adoptive mother. She, too, died of consumption, leaving Poe with a belief in the fatal conjunction of love and death.

John Allan—Poe's adoptive father. He refused to support the struggling poet, and they quarrelled about money.

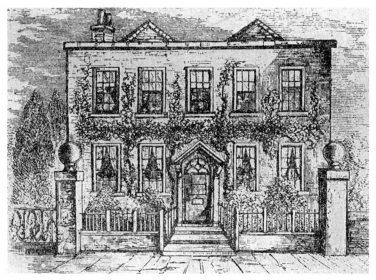

Poe spent part of his childhood in London. He attended Manor House School at Stoke Newington between 1817 and 1820.

But the larger part of Poe's early years was spent in Richmond, Virginia. "Moldavia" was the home of the Allan family and their household slaves.

Elmira Royster at fifteen, sketched by Poe himself in the parlour of the Royster House in Baltimore in 1826. Poe was romantically in love with her, but she gave way to parental pressure and married someone else.

Elmira, now the widowed Mrs. Shelton. In 1849 Poe again paid court to her, but died before anything could come of his renewed attachment.

Watercolour miniature of Poe.

Poe in the early 1840s.

"Muddy," or Maria Clemm, Poe's indomitable aunt and mother-in-law, who kept house for him. She remained devoted to him through poverty, alcoholism, illness, and death.

Street scene in Baltimore.

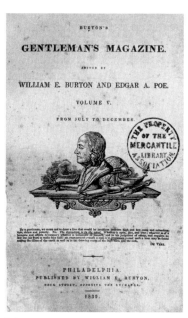

Illustration for "The Gold Bug," Poe's prize-winning story that was published in the Philadelphia Dollar Newspaper *in 1843.*

Title page of Burton's Gentleman's Magazine, *Philadelphia, July 1839. Poe was briefly its editor.*

The Philadelphia market.

Fanny Osgood, one of "The Starry Sisterhood" of wealthy literary ladies who lionised Poe. She dropped him when he caused a scandal by mocking her intimate letters to him.

Poe at about thirty-nine. He is wearing the overcoat he kept from his time as a cadet in the army.

Steamboat en route to New York.

The cottage at Fordham, just outside New York, where Poe's young wife, Virginia, died of consumption in 1847.

Likeness of Virginia, who was propped up in bed for this watercolour to be painted immediately after she died. The picture is somehow both beautiful and macabre, an apt token of Poe's own art.

Annie Richmond.

Helen Whitman.

In a highly emotional state, Poe wrote tender letters to Annie and wild love letters and proposals of marriage to Helen, while dashing from one woman to the other. This photograph was taken in Providence, Rhode Island, on 15 November 1848, four days after he attempted suicide by swallowing an overdose of laudanum.

cursed by lack of success; yet he seemed to some of his contemporaries to be patiently enduring his fate. Stoicism was not the least of his remarkable qualities. Willis also reflected upon "the presence and magnetism of a man of genius" and Poe's "mysterious electricity of mind." But, he added, "he was a man who never smiled."

While staying at the Brennans, earlier that year, Poe had once more been contemplating the prospect of a literary journal. He had been corresponding with such literary men as Charles Anthon, professor of Greek and Latin at Columbia University, on the merits of the scheme. To Anthon he outlined his plan to publish his collected stories in five volumes. He volunteered the fact that "I have reached a crisis of my life, in which I sadly stand in need of aid," and lamented his "long & desperate struggle with the ills attendant upon orphanage, the total want of relatives etcetera." All his old woes had come back, at this low point in his fortunes, but in truth they had never really gone away. He carried them with him everywhere. He might seem cheerful and persevering to his journalistic colleagues, but he harboured a morbid and melancholy mind. Yet even as he complained of "crisis," there came a sudden and overwhelming success.

CHAPTER EIGHT

The Bird

At the beginning of 1845 Poe met a journalistic friend in a New York street and confided in him.

"Wallace," said Poe, "I have just written the greatest poem that ever was written."

"Have you?" replied Wallace. "That is a fine achievement."

"Would you like to hear it?" asked Poe.

"Most certainly," said Wallace.

Thereupon Poe recited the verses of "The Raven." He had been working on it during the period of retreat in the Brennan farmhouse, and he put the last touches to it in the apartment on Greenwich Street. On January 29 it was published in the *Evening Mirror*, and was reprinted in other New York periodicals. It became a sensation. It was his most celebrated poem, and indeed remains one of the most famous poems in American literature:

Once upon a midnight dreary, while I pondered,
  weak and weary,
Over many a quaint and curious volume of forgotten
  lore—
While I nodded, nearly napping, suddenly there came
  a tapping,
As of someone gently rapping, rapping at my chamber door.
" 'Tis some visitor," I muttered, "tapping at my
  chamber door—
Only this and nothing more."

So begins the poem that is a reverie and a lament, a
threnody and a hymn, with its cadences so melodious and
powerful that they still haunt the American poetic imagination. And there is, too, the plangency of the continual
refrain of "Nevermore." The narrator, mourning the
death of a loved one, is visited by the bird of ill omen
whose baleful presence increases his loneliness and desolation. The poem was extolled by one critic as "despair
brooding over wisdom." Poe described the black bird as an
evocation of *"Mournful and Neverending Remembrance."* The
New York Express acclaimed it as surpassing "anything that
has been done even by the best poets of the age," while
the *Richmond Examiner* proclaimed it to have "taken rank
over the whole world of literature." The *New World*, more
plainly, described it as "wild and *shivery*." It was reprinted
ten times, and soon earned the tribute of numerous paro-
dies.

A contemporary noted that "soon the Raven became known everywhere, and everyone was saying 'Nevermore.'" Actors introduced it into their dialogue. It became a catchword. Poe became known as "the Raven," and his habitual appearance in black did not harm the impression. On one occasion he came back to his newspaper office in the company of a then-famous actor. Poe sat at his desk, brought out a manuscript of the poem, and then summoned the entire office to listen to a rendition of the verses by the actor. The office boy recorded that "I was entranced." Poe was soon celebrated in the literary salons of the city, too, and at very little notice he could be prevailed upon to recite the poem in his own particular and mournful manner. He "would turn down the lamps till the room was almost dark," one contemporary remembered, "then standing in the center of the apartment he would recite those wonderful lines in the most melodious of voices . . . So marvellous was his power as a reader that the auditors would be afraid to draw breath lest the enchanted spell be broken."

There are several accounts of his sudden prominence. "Everyone wants to know him," one contemporary wrote, "but only a very few people seem to get well acquainted with him." He appeared at the salons of Miss Lynch on Waverly Place and of Mrs. Smith in Greenwich Street. These literary ladies were known as the "starry sisterhood." He was always neatly dressed, with "the bearing and manners of a gentleman." He was never drunk. He was "polite and engaging . . . quiet and unaffected, unpretentious, in his manner." Virginia Poe would sometimes accompany her husband to these *conversaziones*, as they were known, and demonstrated "the greatest admiration for her husband's genius, and fairly worshipped him." She was not alone. Mrs. Smith revealed that Poe "did not affect the society of men, rather that of highly intellectual women . . . Men were intolerant of all this, but women fell under his fascination and listened in silence." They recognised his need, perhaps, and his orphan's sense of privation. One specimen of his conversation has been preserved in the diary of Mrs. Smith:

> "Ah Mr. Poe, this country affords no arena for those who live to dream."
> "Do you dream? I mean sleeping dream?"
> "Oh yes, I am a perfect Joseph in dreaming, except that my dreams are of the unknown, the spiritual."
> "I knew it. I knew it by your eyes."

Poe was no doubt delighted by the acclaim and attention. He had always wished for fame and now, in a way he had found it. "No man lives," he is once reported to have said, "unless he is famous." He also enjoyed being praised. Nevertheless he contrived to be somewhat ironical about the poem's success. "The Raven has had a great 'run,' Thomas," he wrote to Frederick Thomas, "—but I wrote it for the express purpose of running—just as I did the 'Gold-Bug' you know. The bird beat the bug, though, all hollow." The tone of calculation here is thoroughly familiar. He was writing poetry exactly as most people perceived poetry to be. He was writing poetry for a specific market. He told a journalistic colleague that he wished "to see how near to the absurd I could come without overstepping the dividing line."

Poe even wrote an essay, "The Philosophy of Composition," in which he outlined the principles of his art and provided an anatomy of the poem stanza by stanza. He set down the proper length of a poem, and the most appropriate tone of "sadness"; he elucidated the required "effects," and the importance of a significant refrain. He stated that the work proceeded, step by step, to its completion with the precision and rigid consequence of a mathematical problem. "It was a thoroughly methodical and technical handbook for the writing of a great poem. In the course of this supposedly objective analysis he announced that "the death, then, of a beautiful woman is, unquestionably, the most poetic topic in the world" without revealing his reasons for the choice. He set down, in order, his tricks and devices; it was a need for orderliness, similar to that which had sent him into the Army and West Point.

This apparently cynical and impersonal account, however, should be placed beside the confession to a friend that reciting the poem "set his brain on fire." What remains is not its technical audacity, or its melodic control, but the horror of its morbid despair. Poe's impersonality resembles the apparent calmness of the frenzied narrators of his stories.

. . .

In the flush of success he left his post as "para-graphist" on the *Evening Mirror* and joined the rival *Broadway Journal*, where he began to reprint some of his earlier published tales and poems. He also continued a round of literary hostilities, initiated in the *Evening Mirror*, in which he attacked the poetry and reputation of Henry Wadsworth Longfellow. Longfellow was at this time one of the senior poetic figures in America, but his status was only likely to excite Poe's wrath. Poe reviewed an anthology edited by Longfellow, *The Waif*, and accused the older poet of excluding any poets deemed to rival Longfellow himself; he also accused him of gross and obvious plagiarism. He described him as a "determined imitator and a dexterous adapter of the ideas of other people," and denounced him for plagiarism of Tennyson that was "too palpable to be mistaken . . . [and] which belongs to the most barbarous class of literary robbery."

It was in part a means of providing "copy" for his new journal. But it was also a ploy to provoke public attention; he even went so far as to compose an imaginary riposte to his own charges, under the name of "Outis," or "Nobody," simply to continue the public debate for a little longer. He succeeded in that, at least, and the onesided battle between Poe and Longfellow rendered it one of the most famous literary feuds in American literary history. Poe's writing on the subject amounted to one hundred pages. He compounded the offence by lecturing at the New York Society Library on "Poets and Poetry of America." This had been the title he had given to his lecture a year before, but on this occasion he broadened his assault by including Longfellow and in particular his "fatal alacrity at imitation." Longfellow never deigned to reply to his accuser's charges in public, but he commented later that Poe's attacks upon him had been provoked by "the irritation of a sensitive nature chafed by some indefinite sense of wrong." In that diagnosis he was probably correct.

Poe was not only executioner in chief on the *Broadway Journal*. He was also its theatrical critic. He was not a benign one, and one theatrical manager withdrew Poe's name from the free list of critics after a particularly vicious review of his company's *Antigone*.

The office boy, Alexander Crane, remembered that Poe was "a quiet man about the office, but was uniformly kind and courteous to everyone, and, with congenial company, he would grow cheerful and even playful." He arrived at nine each morning, and worked "steadily and methodically" until three or four in the afternoon. On one occasion Crane fainted in the heat, and revived to discover Poe "bending over me bathing my wrists and temples in cold water." So he was considerate as well as courteous.

. . .

But the move from the relative seclusion of the farmhouse, and the excitement derived from the reception of "The Raven," once more propelled him towards drink.

Alexander Crane recalled that, the morning after one of his lectures had been cancelled as a result of bad weather, he came into the office "leaning on the arm of a friend, intoxicated with wine." He had obviously been drinking all night. A New York magazine presented a fictitious list of forthcoming books, with one entitled "A treatise on 'Aqua Pura,' its uses and abuses, by Edgar A Poe." So his drinking habits were well known.

He had been asked to prepare a poem for recitation at a society of New York University, but found that he could not perform the task. He became worried about this failure and, according to Thomas Dunn English, "as he always does when troubled—drank until intoxicated; and remained in a state of intoxication during the week." The records of his drunken "sprees," as he used to call them, suggest that New York was not the proper place for him. He informed one acquaintance that he was about to recite "The Raven" to Queen Victoria and the royal family. He told him, also, that other writers were conspiring against him. So the over-indulgence in alcohol could lead him perilously close to madness.

A colleague, Thomas Holley Chivers, walking down Nassau Street, recognised him "tottering from side to side, as drunk as an Indian." When Poe saw Chivers he cried out, "By God! Here is my friend now! Where are you going? Come, you must go home with me." He became generally over-excited and, seeing a rival editor across the street a few minutes later, was barely restrained by Chivers from attacking him. Chivers then escorted him home. When Virginia saw them from an upstairs window, she retreated into her room and locked the door. Maria Clemm greeted her errant son-in-law, according to Chivers, with a refrain of "Oh! Eddy! Eddy! Eddy! Come here, my dear boy. Let me put you to bed." She also apparently confided to Chivers, "I do believe that the poor boy is deranged!" It is clear enough that Virginia, wasting from day to day, could not bear to see her husband in this condition. She may even have believed that Poe's despair at her illness helped to provoke his heavy drinking. She may just have been too frail to cope with her husband's frantic and tiresome behaviour. According to Chivers, Maria Clemm lamented the illness of her daughter, with the claim that "the Doctors can do her no good. But if they could, seeing this continually in poor Eddy, would kill her . . . would to God that she had died before she had ever seen him." The memory of Maria Clemm's words may not be altogether accurate, but she was clearly blaming Poe in part for Virginia's suffering. Another colleague wrote in a diary entry at this time, "There is Poe with coolness, immaculate personal cleanliness, sensitiveness, the gentleman, continually putting himself on a level with the lowest blackguard through a combination of moral, mental and physical drunkenness."

Poe knew as much himself, and in the summer of 1845 *Graham's Magazine* published his "The Imp of the Perverse." It was a narrative of rueful contemplation in which the narrator muses upon the human capacity to act in a contrary manner "for the reason that we should *not*." To do that which is forbidden—to do that which goes against all our instincts of self-love and self-preservation—therein lies the power of the imp. Never to stay long in any employment; to be drawn towards young women who were dying; to quarrel continually with friends; to drink excessively, even when told that the indulgence would kill him. Therein dwells the imp.

. . .

James Russell Lowell, a young poet of considerable gifts, visited the Poe household during this spring and summer of 1845. Some months before, Lowell had written a long and favourable criticism of Poe's work for *Graham's Magazine*, in which he gave the opinion that "we know of none who has displayed more varied and more striking abilities." It was the first long article about Poe that had not been deliberately engineered by Poe himself. There had been a correspondence between the two writers, and Lowell already considered Poe to be a "dear friend." But their encounter was not altogether a success. Poe was "a little tipsy, as if he were recovering from a fit of drunkenness." He seemed to Lowell to be in an unhappy and sarcastic mood. His manner was "rather formal, even pompous." He was not at his best. Lowell noticed, too, that Poe's ailing wife had an "anxious expression." (Five years later Maria Clemm wrote to apologise to

Lowell, informing him that "the day you saw him in New York he was not himself.") But then Poe attacked Lowell's poetry in print, and even accused him of plagiarising material from Wordsworth. Lowell retaliated by suggesting that Poe was bereft of "that element of manhood which, for want of a better name, we call character." Poe was weak, in other words.

But what was his character, in the most general sense? He has alternately been described as ambitious and unworldly, jealous and restrained, childlike and theatrical, fearful and vicious, self-confident and wayward, defiant and self-pitying. He was all of these, and more. One acquaintance described him as "unstable as water," and another as a "characterless character." To one who became his enemy he was "the merest shell of a man."

Like the salamander he could only live in fire. But the fire was often started by himself. He stumbled from one passionate outburst to the next. He hardly seemed to know himself at all, but relied upon the power of impassioned words to create his identity. He would sometimes tear at himself, heaping misery upon himself, estranging others even while realising that it was wrong to do so. He moved from disaster to calamity and back again. His entire life was a series of mistakes and setbacks, of disappointed hopes and thwarted ambitions. He proceeded as if he were the only one in the world—hence the spitefulness of his criticism. He drew attention to his solitary state in defiance and celebration, even as he lamented it in his letters. Thus, at the centre of his work, was anger against the world. He had a heart always about to break.

There was a curious incident in the summer of 1845 that justified the bad opinions that some held of him. A young poet, R.H. Stoddard, had submitted a poem for the *Broadway Journal.* Having received no reply, he sought out Poe at his lodgings. Poe then assured him that the poem would appear in the next number of the periodical, but it did not. Instead there was a notice: "To the author of the lines on the 'Grecian Flute.' We fear that we have mislaid the poem." Then, in the following month, another "notice" appeared, to Stoddard's astonishment, remarking that "we doubt the originality of the 'Grecian Flute,' for the reason that it is too good at some points to be so bad at others." This is the authentic Poe tone. In dismay Stoddard visited the offices of the *Journal,* to encounter Poe "irascible, surly and in his cups." Poe stared up "wildly" at the unfortunate young poet, and then accused him of plagiarism. "You never wrote the Ode to which I lately referred." He abused Stoddard and, in the young man's words, threatened him "with condign personal chastisement"—that is, a thrashing—and ordered him to leave the office.

In this period Poe was professing himself once more to be depressed and "dreadfully unwell, and fear that I shall be very seriously ill." The household had been regularly moving lodgings—from Greenwich Street to East Broadway and from East Broadway to Amity Street near

Washington Square. But now Poe resolved to return to the countryside, in order to regain his health and his composure, and as a result wished to give up his post on the *Broadway Journal.* He was trying to sell his "interest" in the newspaper. His partner, Charles Frederick Briggs, was not unhappy to see him leave. Poe's drinking had made him unreliable. "I shall haul down Poe's name," he wrote. "He has lately got into his old habits and I fear will injure himself irretrievably." But then Poe changed his mind. He had told Thomas Dunn English that the "comparative failure" of the *Journal* was a consequence of "the fact that he had it not all in his own hands." He is reported to have said, "Give me the entire control, and it will be the great literary journal of the future." So he had transferred his hopes for an ideal literary magazine to the *Broadway Journal* itself.

In the summer of 1845, too, there appeared a volume of twelve stories by Poe. *Tales* was published by the New York firm of Wiley and Putnam, and included "The Murders in the Rue Morgue" and "The Black Cat." If it was an attempt to capitalise on the fame Poe had achieved with "The Raven," it succeeded in part. The small volume was praised by the *American Review* as "one of the most original and peculiar ever published in the United States," and by *Graham's Magazine* as "among the most original and characteristic compositions in American letters." Of all the books published in Poe's lifetime, it was the most successful. Four months after publication, according to his own estimate, it had sold approximately fifteen hundred copies, thus earning Poe a royalty of over one hundred dollars. It was not munificent, but it was gratefully received.

. . .

In July he made an unexpected trip to Providence, Rhode Island, for which he had to borrow ten dollars from a friend. It was a secret journey, which he could not finance with the help of Maria Clemm. Poe had in mind a form of assignation.

In one of his drunken fits he had divulged that he was involved "in the damnedst amour." His wife, of course, was not to be told. The lady in question was Mrs. Frances Osgood, a literary "blue-stocking" (or "blue," as the race was known), who composed verses and tales for New York periodicals. Poe had praised "Fanny" Osgood in his lecture on American poets, and eventually met her in the drawing room of the Astor Hotel in New York. She recalled the meeting at a later date with all the enhanced recollection of hindsight. "With his proud and beautiful head erect," she said, "his dark eyes flashing with the elective light of feeling and thought, a peculiar, an inimitable blend of sweetness and hauteur in his expression and manner, he greeted me calmly, gravely, almost coldly . . ."

The coldness must soon have vanished, however. They exchanged verses, and Poe printed several of her poems in the *Broadway Journal*. It was a highly public and publicised romance, if romance it was. It is more likely to have been a fussy and excitable literary friendship, lent added fervour by Poe's desperate need for the comfort and protection of women. They exchanged letters as well as verses, but the correspondence has since been lost. Poe's poems to her were not necessarily inspired by passionate devotion. One poem, "To F————S O————D," had in fact been written for Virginia eleven years before; another tribute, "To F," had been written in 1835 at which stage it was composed "To Mary." He was not averse to recycling his emotions.

Frances Osgood's New York publisher recalled that "when she was with my family, Poe called every day and generally spent the evening remaining invariably until midnight." She was often present at the literary parties to which Poe was now a frequent visitor. Another writer recalled "the child-like face of Fannie Osgood suffused with tears under his [Poe's] wizard spell." Thomas Dunn English also described "little Mrs. Osgood doing the infantile act . . . her face upturned to Poe." She clearly had an advanced case of literary hero-worship, a form of adoration that Poe did his best to maintain. He courted her a little too ardently, however, and Mrs. Osgood described at a later date how "I went to Albany, and afterwards to Boston and Providence to avoid him." She added that "he followed me to each of these places and wrote to me, imploring me to love him." It sounds very much like a long pursued affair except for the fact that Mrs. Osgood's husband, the painter Samuel Osgood, was well aware of their association. Possibly it was an innocent, or unthreatening, dalliance. Adultery was not then generally acceptable, even in New York.

. . .

When Fanny Osgood visited the Poe household in New York, she found him working on a series of papers entitled "The Literati of New York." He always wrote on narrow strips of paper, pasted into long rolls, and on this occasion he showed the various lengths of them to Fanny. His wife was present at the time. "Come, Virginia," Mrs. Osgood remembered him saying, "help me!" Together they unrolled each piece until "at last they came to one which seemed interminable. Virginia laughingly ran to one corner of the room with one end and her husband to the opposite with the other." Mrs. Osgood asked about whom this effusion was written. "Hear her," he said, "just as if that little vain heart didn't tell her it's herself!" It is a mawkish episode, not relieved by the fact that Poe did indeed compose rather nauseous tributes to Mrs. Osgood's poetry. He had no steadiness in critical matters. He was swayed by private passion and personal rivalry. The fact that Fanny Osgood visited husband and wife, however, reinforces the impression that Fanny and Poe were not engaged in any sexual relationship. It seems that Mrs. Poe even asked Mrs. Osgood to continue her correspondence with Poe, on the grounds that their friendship helped to keep him sober. He found comfort in Fanny Osgood.

It is significant that, in one character portrait of her,

Poe described her "hair black and glossy: eyes a clear, luminous gray, large, and with singular capacity for expression." This might be a description of one of the doomed women of his tales. It might almost be a description of his mother. Four years later, Fanny Osgood did indeed die of consumption. Could he have already noticed the signs of it upon her—he was preternaturally sensitive to such things—and thus have been drawn to her?

Margaret Fuller, the most dispassionate and most intelligent of his observers, believed that his love affairs were in truth part of a "passionate illusion, which he amused himself by inducing, than of sympathy." She believed that he had no friends, and that he was "shrouded in an assumed character." It is possible that he was indeed playing a part, taking on a Byronic aspect for the sake of his female admirers, but was at the same time desperate and unbalanced. He became the part, living it with an intensity that belied its artificial nature.

. . .

Throughout the summer of 1845 he was working sporadically upon a book of poems. *The Raven and Other Poems* would be the first such collection since 1831. It was a significant publication, therefore, not least because he believed that he would earn five hundred dollars from its sales. His hopes were, as always, unfulfilled. He chose some thirty poems for the collection, among them such early works as "Tamerlane" and "Al Aaraaf." In a preface he declared that "events not to be controlled have prevented me from making, at any time, any serious effort in what, under happier circumstances, would have been the field of my choice. With me poetry has been not a purpose, but a passion." Unfortunately, the critics were not as well disposed towards the poems as to the tales. And the volume did not sell. It would be the last collection of Poe's poetry in his lifetime.

He professed to be abstaining from alcohol, or "the ashes" as he called it, but by the autumn he was drinking again. He was always prone to spectacular miscalculations about the effect of his behaviour, and a reading in Boston proved to be what one critic has described as the beginning of his "downfall." He had been invited to read at the event, in order to celebrate a new series of lectures in the Boston Lyceum. He was called upon to recite a new work at the end of a lecture by a Massachusetts politician, Caleb Cushing, but spent "some fifteen minutes with an apology for not delivering, as is usual in such cases, a didactic poem." Poe did not write didactic poems; for him poetry and didacticism were antithetical. Poetry was concerned with the pursuit of the "beautiful" only—what was for him "supernal beauty" or "the beauty above."

This was the stirring message he delivered to the Bostonians. One Harvard student, present at the occasion, recalled that "he stood with a sort of shrinking before the audience and then began in a thin, tremulous, hardly musical voice, an apology for his poem, and a deprecation of the expected criticism of a Boston audience." The student also noticed his "look of oversensitiveness which when uncontrolled may prove more debasing than coarseness." Poe was, in other words, nervous and expecting the worst from a difficult group. Then he proceeded to recite "Al Aaraaf," a poem that he had written sixteen years previously. Some of his auditors grew restive under the strain of understanding this juvenile performance, and so Poe was prevailed upon to read "The Raven" at the close of the proceedings. Members of the audience, however, were already leaving with much noisy vacating of seats.

It was not a particularly glorious night, but then Poe, over "a bottle of champagne," compounded the offence by revealing to some Bostonian writers and journalists that "Al Aaraaf" was indeed a poem of his youth. They were not pleased by the intelligence, assuming it to be an insult both to Boston and to the Lyceum. The editor of the *Boston Evening Transcript*, Cornelia Wells Walter, disclosed that the poem had been composed *"before its author was twelve years old."* Poe, in one of his flights of fancy, may even have stated this improbable fact. Miss Walter continued in a vein of thinly concealed sarcasm, "a poem delivered before a literary association of adults, as written by a boy! Only think of it! Poh! Poh!" He retaliated in kind. "Well, upon the whole we must forgive her," he wrote, "—and do. Say no more about it, you little darling!" The last expression was considered to be unwholesome.

It should be remembered that Poe was a Southerner.

He was a Virginian, if not by birth, at least by inclination. He disliked the culture of New England in general, and of Boston in particular; he despised in equal measure Transcendentalism and Abolitionism. He was in spirit if not in practice a Southern gentleman. That accounts for the somewhat florid classicism, and the melodic intensity, of his prose. "It is high time," he once wrote, "that the literary South took its own interests into its own charge." So in Boston he had entered the den of his enemies.

He retaliated to the resulting abuse by proudly claiming to have "quizzed," or made fun of, the Bostonians. In the *Broadway Journal* Poe revealed that "we like Boston. We were born there—and perhaps it is just as well not to mention that we are heartily ashamed of the fact . . . the Bostonians have no soul." He added salt to the wound, or fuel to the flame, by adding that "it *could* scarcely be supposed that we would put ourselves to the trouble of composing for the Bostonians anything in the shape of an original poem . . . it did well enough for a Boston audience." This was, at the very least, ungracious.

Cornelia Walter herself then returned to the attack by noting that "it must be confessed that he did *out-Yankee* the managers of the Lyceum since he not only emptied their pockets but emptied the house." The general impression, assiduously spread by Miss Walter and others, was of Poe as unreliable and discourteous. He was not serious. He was a charlatan and a drunkard.

. . .

In this inauspicious month Poe also took charge of the *Broadway Journal*. In a series of negotiations and schemings he bought out his erstwhile partners. "By a flurry of manoeuvres almost incomprehensible to myself," he wrote, "I have succeeded, one by one, in getting rid, one by one, of all my associates." He also raised funds from friends and even issued an advertisement in the *Journal* itself proclaiming "A RARE OPPORTUNITY" for an investment in the enterprise. He begged money, he borrowed money, he promised money. Then, on 25 October 1845, Poe's name was blazoned on the masthead of the *Journal* as "Editor and Proprietor." "I have to do *everything myself*," he wrote, "edit the paper—get it to press—and attend to the multitudinous *business* besides."

One of his erstwhile partners, Charles Frederick Briggs, was happy to relinquish any interest in the magazine. He regarded Poe as a liability, calling him "the merest shell of a man," "a drunken sot," and the "most purely selfish of human beings." He added for good measure that Poe quoted from the German without being able to understand a word of the language. This is likely to have been true. Briggs also believed that, in retaliation, Poe was spreading lies about him in New York: "I cannot conceive of such wanton malice, as Poe has been guilty of towards me."

As sole proprietor, Poe was not a success. He curtailed the coverage of the *Journal*, for want of funds, and could not afford to pay any decent contributors. He republished his own work, and printed the poems of the "starry sisterhood" and other poetasters. The magazine's circulation was uneven, and its publication was fitful. Six weeks after acquiring the editorship he sold half of his interest to Thomas H. Lane, a Customs House employee he had met in Philadelphia. "For the first time during two months," he told one acquaintance, "I find myself entirely myself— dreadfully sick and depressed, but still myself. I seem to have just awakened from some horrible dream . . . I really believe that I have been mad." He had been "mad" at the Lyceum, "mad" in his pursuit of Mrs. Osgood, "mad" in his decision to take up the editorship of the *Journal.* The madness, if such it was, had come from the combined effects of drink and intolerable strain. A month after signing the agreement with Lane, according to English, Poe succumbed to "one of his drunken sprees." Lane closed down the magazine on 3 January 1846. It was the last editorial position Poe would ever hold.

The day before the *Broadway Journal* closed Poe witnessed an agreement by which Maria Clemm relinquished her claim to a piece of Baltimore property, worth twenty-five dollars; the family must have been desperate indeed to sign away their last piece of capital.

In the previous November Stoddard had passed Poe in the street. It was raining heavily, and for a moment Stoddard considered sharing his umbrella with him. But "something—certainly not unkindness—withheld me. I went on and left him there in the rain, pale, shivering, miserable . . . There I still see him, and always shall,— poor, penniless, but proud, reliant, dominant." In the same month Poe wrote to a relation, George Poe, "I have perseveringly struggled, against a thousand difficulties, and have succeeded, although not in making money, still in attaining a position in the world of Letters, of which, under the circumstances, I have no reason to be ashamed."

CHAPTER NINE

The Scandal

Poe believed that he had many enemies. He blamed the failure of the *Broadway Journal* "on the part of one or two persons who are much imbittered against me," and he declared that "there is a deliberate attempt now being made to involve me in ruin." It is not clear who these "one or two persons" were, if they existed at all, but they may have been rival newspaper editors or writers unhappy about Poe's often scathing critical notices. But he was right to sense persecution. At the beginning of 1846, he was involved in unwelcome scandal. It came from an unexpected quarter.

In his life there were certain literary females who vied for his attention. Principal among them were Elizabeth F. Ellet, Fanny Osgood, Margaret Fuller, and Anne Lynch. Fanny Osgood, the poetess of New York, was by now a family friend. Margaret Fuller was a writer and reviewer who, four years before, had edited a Transcendentalist quarterly the *Dial*; she had met Poe at a soirée in New York. Anne Lynch was a poetess and teacher, who hosted some of these soirées. Elizabeth Ellet was a poet and novelist whose work Poe had printed and praised in the *Broadway Journal*. Fanny Osgood, in perhaps not the most charitable spirit, remarked that Elizabeth Ellet "followed him everywhere."

Elizabeth Ellet and Fanny Osgood had written rapturous letters to Poe that, to a prurient reader, might have erred on the side of indiscretion. Expressions of poetic devotion, as he himself knew well enough, are not the same thing as true passion. Yet that is not how it seemed at the time, when the two women became incensed and then alarmed at the manner in which their missives were being treated.

Early in 1846, Mrs. Ellet decided one day to call upon Poe at his home in Amity Street. When she came up to the house, she heard laughter, and on gaining entrance discovered Fanny Osgood in the parlour with Virginia Poe. It soon became evident that they were laughing at a letter. It was still in Fanny Osgood's hand, and it was Mrs. Ellet's letter to Poe. Mrs. Ellet snatched it up, and marched out. That is one version.

There is another. Mrs. Ellet called at Amity Street and, in the course of her visit, Virginia read out to her a letter to Poe from Mrs. Osgood. (If this version of the story is true, it is difficult to know why Virginia was being indiscreet.) Mrs. Ellet professed to be somewhat alarmed by the tone of Mrs. Osgood's letter. No doubt aching with excitement, she went immediately to see Mrs. Osgood herself to advise her to retrieve all her letters to Poe. The question was one of womanly modesty.

The two other literary ladies now entered the scene. Margaret Fuller and Anne Lynch, dear friends from the soirées, visited Poe and formally demanded the return of Mrs. Osgood's letters. Poe was naturally resentful. He responded that Fanny Osgood was not alone. Elizabeth Ellet's letters were also open to misinterpretation.

In the meantime Elizabeth Ellet had asked her brother to call upon Poe and demanded the return of her letters. Poe insisted to him that he had already sent them back to Mrs. Ellet. But the brother did not believe him and threatened to kill him if he did not produce them. Poe then visited Thomas Dunn English, and asked for the use of his pistol. English denied the request, and insinuated that Poe never did possess any letters from Mrs. Ellet in the first place. The two men engaged in some kind of tussle. It sounds like the most absurd fiction, but somewhere in the welter of claim and counter-claim there was a genuine imbroglio.

Poe retreated to his bed after his encounter with English, and then persuaded his physician to deliver an apologetic letter to Mrs. Ellet. He denied making any improper claims about her correspondence but added that, if he did make any such remarks, he must have been suffering from temporary insanity. Mrs. Osgood was also incensed about the mockery of her own letters, and persuaded Virginia Poe to write her a letter confirming what she called "my innocence."

Poe never saw Elizabeth Ellet, or Fanny Osgood, again. Mrs. Ellet declared him to be "steeped in infamy." He was ostracised from the salons of the starry sisterhood. According to Anne Lynch, Poe "said & did a great many things that were very abominable." At a later date he was to excoriate "the pestilential society of *literary women*. They are a heartless, unnatural, venomous, dishonorable *set*, with no guiding principle but inordinate self-esteem."

Anne Lynch described him as having "no moral sense." It should be added that his stories have no "moral sense," either, and that he disdained any such principle. Is "moral sense" to be expected of the man rather than the writer?

. . .

Yet his appetite for controversy was not extinguished. During this period a friend and journalist, William Gilmore Simms, wrote to him that "you are now perhaps in the most perilous period of your career—just in that position—just at that time of life—when a false step becomes a capital error—when a single leading mistake is fatal in its consequences." Poe was not one to listen to advice, however well meant; nor was he ever likely to learn from his mistakes. His presiding deity was, after all, the imp of the perverse.

And so, perversely, in the spring of 1846, he began a

series of essays for *Godey's Lady's Book* entitled "The Literati of New York: Some Honest Opinions at Random Respecting their Authorial Merits, with Occasional Words of Personality." Poe was in fact planning to bring out a volume of critical essays, entitled *The American Parnassus*, and these sketches were the first airing of a number of pieces, critical or respectful, on the merits of the more celebrated authors of the day. He resented the undue praise and "puffery" expended on what he considered to be "unworthy" writers and, as a result, he could at times be exceedingly satirical. Indeed he launched a full-scale attack on the literary cliques and circles that controlled the publication and reception of American literature; they represented what he called "the corrupt nature of our ordinary criticism."

Of Lewis Gaylord Clark, the editor of the *Knickerbocker*, Poe wrote that "as a literary man, he has about him no determinateness, no distinctiveness, no point—an apple, in fact, or a pumpkin has more angles . . . he is noticeable for nothing in the world except for the markedness by which he is noticeable for nothing." Of Thomas Dunn English, erstwhile friend but now confirmed enemy, Poe wrote that "I do not personally know him." This false denial was followed up by a swipe at English's appearance: "he exists in a perpetual state of vacillation between moustachio and goatee." Poe excelled at this kind of ad hominem criticism; it was immensely readable at the time, of course, with three editions of some issues being printed to keep up with sales. Poe was the most controversial, and most widely discussed, literary journalist in the country. It is not clear, however, that his reputation as a writer was improved.

Some of his victims also had an unfortunate habit of fighting back. Lewis Gaylord Clark retorted, in the *Knickerbocker*, that Poe was "a wretched inebriate" and a "jaded hack." He quoted from an unnamed source, most likely Clark himself, that "he called at our office the other day, in a condition of sad imbecility, bearing in his feeble body the evidences of evil living and betrayed by his talk such radical obliquity of sense . . . He was accompanied by an aged female relative who was going a weary round in the hot streets, following his steps to prevent his indulging in a love of drink; but he had eluded her watchful eye by some means, and was already far gone in a state of inebriation."

There was worse to come. Thomas Dunn English also responded in kind with an attack upon Poe in the *New York Mirror*, in which severe remarks about his personal appearance were mingled with more serious charges; English accused Poe of forgery, of acquiring money under false pretences and of plagiarism. Poe promptly sued the *Mirror* for libel.

He had already removed himself from the city. The streets were too treacherous, and offered too many temptations. The tranquillity and purer air of the countryside were also deemed necessary for Virginia Poe's slowly fading health. In February the Poe household settled near the East River. A nine-year-old neighbour recalled how Poe would "run over every little while to ask my father to lend him our rowboat, and then how he would enjoy himself pulling at the oars over to the little islands just south of Blackwell's Island, for his afternoon swim." Poe loved the water. The girl added that "I never liked him. I was afraid of him. But I liked Mrs. Clemm, she was a splendid woman, a great talker and fully aware of 'Eddie's failings'—as she called them." Of Virginia Poe she remembered that she was "pale and delicate" but "patient in her suffering." The little girl recalled Virginia talking to Poe. "Now, Eddie," she said, "when I am gone I will be your guardian angel, and if at any time you feel tempted to do wrong, just put your hands above your head, so, and I will be there to shield you." It is a sad remembrance.

. . .

Four months later the Poe family moved further out to Fordham, a village thirteen miles to the north of New York, where they found a small cottage half-buried in blossom and fruit trees. Virginia was "charmed" by the place, according to Poe, and they rented the property "for a very trifling sum." The house faced west. There were lilac bushes, and a cherry tree, in the small front garden, while beyond were apple orchards and a wood. It was to be their last home on earth together. It was, as always, an impoverished one. Maria Clemm resorted to digging up the turnips meant for the cattle. She was seen gathering dandelions and other greens in the country lanes to make up a palatable salad. "Greens," she used to tell neighbours, "are cooling for the blood. Eddie's fond of them." But Eddie had little choice in the matter.

The not infrequent callers would bring baskets of produce for the family. Maria Clemm was also in the habit of "borrowing" money from their visitors. Since some of these visitors were aspiring writers there were occasions when Poe would be obliged to repay their generosity with little "puffs" of his own in the public prints. Maria Clemm seems to have managed the business very well.

There are small glimpses of life at Fordham. A neighbour was passing their cottage, one morning, when she saw Poe picking cherries from the tree and throwing them down to Virginia. But then she saw that Virginia's white dress was "dashed with blood as bright as the cherries she had caught." She would never forget the expression on Poe's face as he carried his wife into the cottage. "They were awful poor," she said. Maria Clemm wrote that it "was the sweetest little cottage imaginable. Oh, how supremely happy we were in our dear cottage home! We three lived only for each other. Eddie rarely left his beautiful home. I attended to his literary business; for he, poor fellow, knew nothing about money transactions."

He could not, however, wholly escape the attentions of the city. Fordham was on the Harlem Railroad, running from Williamsbridge to City Hall, and the trains departed every four hours. Certainly he was in New York on one evening in June 1846, because he composed a letter to his wife on a piece of pocket notebook paper. "My dear

Heart," he began. He hoped that "the interview I am promised, will result in some *substantial good* for me . . . in my last great disappointment, I should have lost my courage *but for you*." The nature of the "interview," and of the "disappointment," are not known. He added that "my darling wife you are my *greatest* and *only* stimulus now. To battle with this uncongenial, unsatisfactory and ungrateful life."

It had become uncongenial in every sense. There had already been rumours circulating in the public prints about Poe's "insanity." According to the *Saturday Visiter* of Baltimore, in April, Poe "labors under mental derangement, to such a degree that it has been determined to consign him to the Insane Retreat at Utica." These tales were the direct result of the unfortunate letter Poe had persuaded his doctor to write, on the subject of the correspondence with Mrs. Ellet, in which he had claimed that he was suffering from a fit of temporary insanity. As the news of his explanation spread, so did the gossip.

The gossip was fanned by the libel suit he was still pursuing. He was suing the *New York Mirror,* which had published English's claims of forgery and plagiarism. Poe's lawyer submitted a suit for libel in the Superior Court of New York, claiming that Poe's "good name, fame and credit" had been wilfully injured; he demanded damages of five thousand dollars. The case was put back, and then put back again, but the coverage of the New York journals was generally hostile to Poe. "This is rather small business," commented the New York *Morning News,* "for a man who has reviled nearly every literary man of eminence in the United States."

Poe was now physically, if not mentally, unstable. He was forced to turn down a commencement event at the University of Vermont, as a result of "serious and, I fear, permanent ill health." One newspaper interpreted this as "brain fever." It is as good an explanation as any. That summer, from the cottage at Fordham, he wrote a long letter to Chivers in which he confessed that "I have been for a long time dreadfully ill." He spoke of those intending to "ruin" him. "My dreadful poverty," he wrote, "also, has given them every advantage. In fact, my dear friend, I have been driven to the very gates of death and a despair more dreadful than death . . ." So did fate choose to pursue Poe throughout his life.

He and his household now also became the object of sustained press attention. On 15 December 1846, the New York *Morning Express* carried an item headlined ILLNESS OF EDGAR A. POE. "We regret to learn," the journalist wrote, "that this gentleman and his wife are both dangerously ill with the consumption, and that the hand of misfortune lies heavy upon their temporal affairs—We are sorry to mention the fact that they are so far reduced as to be barely able to obtain the necessaries of life." The same facts were reprinted, with one or two embellishments, in several other newspapers. Even the *Mirror*, against which he had issued the libel writ, came to his aid with an appeal for contributions. Money was indeed taken up on the family's behalf. One newspaper editor collected fifty or sixty dollars, and anonymous donors sent gifts of ten dollars or more.

Poe was alternately grateful and resentful. He needed the money, clearly, but he did not like to be paraded as an object of public charity. Nor was he pleased that his wife's mortal illness was also being publicised. At the end of the year he sent one newspaper editor a letter in which he regretted the fact that "the concerns of my family are thus pitilessly thrust before the public." He claimed "that I have ever materially suffered from privation, beyond the extent of my capacity for suffering, is not altogether true. That I am 'without friends' is a gross calumny . . ." (Friendlessness was a condition about which he had often complained.) He added that "even in the city of New York I could have no difficulty in naming a hundred persons" to whom he could apply for aid without humiliation. He concluded the letter with a defiant declaration. "The truth is, I have a great deal to do; and I have made up my mind not to die till it is done." He did in fact protest too much, and admitted later that his exculpatory words had put him to "the expense of truth at denying those necessities which were but too real."

They were real enough to enlist the active help and sympathy of some New York ladies who had become aware of the Poes' plight during the late autumn and winter of 1846. One of them, Mrs. Gove-Nichols, recalled seeing Virginia Poe lying on a straw bed "wrapped in her husband's greatcoat, with a large tortoise shell cat in her bosom. The wonderful cat seemed conscious of her great usefulness. The coat and the cat were the sufferer's only means of warmth, except as her husband held her hands and her mother her feet." She informed a friend, Mrs. Shew, who promptly organised a subscription for the unhappy family. A feather bed and bed clothing were supplied, followed by a gift of sixty dollars.

By the beginning of 1847 it was clear that Virginia Poe was failing. She had said to a caller, "I know I shall die soon; I know I can't get well; but I want to be as happy as possible, and make Edgar happy." She suffered from fever and sweating, an inability to draw breath, and severe chest pain, spitting of blood and perpetual coughing. These had also been the symptoms of Poe's ailing mother. Indeed Virginia Poe died at the same age as Eliza Poe. The fatal coincidence could not have been lost upon Poe himself. A visitor to Fordham, in these last months of her life, found him "lost in a stupor, not living or suffering, but existing merely." Maria Clemm recalled that Poe "was devoted to her till the last hour of her life, as his friends can testify." But, in addition, the distress of Maria Clemm herself was "dreadful to see."

Friends and relations gathered at the little cottage in Fordham. Among them was Poe's old acquaintance from Baltimore, Mary Devereaux, now Mrs. Jennings. She found the dying woman seated in the parlour. "I said to her, 'Do you feel any better today?' and sat down by the big armchair in which she was placed. Mr. Poe sat on the other side of her. I had my hand in hers, and she took it and placed it in Mr. Poe's, saying 'Mary, be a friend to Eddie and don't forsake him.' " That evening Poe wrote a letter to his benefactress, Mrs. Shew, observing that "My poor Virginia still lives, although fading fast and now suffering much pain . . . Lest she may never see you more— she bids me say that she sends you her sweetest kiss of love and will die blessing you." And he added, "Yes, I *will* be calm."

The next morning, 30 January 1847, Mary Devereaux returned to Fordham, accompanied by Mrs. Shew. Virginia was still just alive, and gave Mrs. Shew a portrait of Poe together with a jewel box that had been owned by Poe's sister, Rosalie.

Virginia expired soon after. It was then realised that no portrait of her existed, and so one of the ladies quickly finished a watercolour of her likeness. It survives still.

Mrs. Shew had purchased a shroud of fine linen. On the day of the funeral the coffin was placed on Virginia's husband's desk, beside which she had so often sat in the past. It was a bitterly cold day. Poe, wrapped in the greatcoat he had owned since his days at West Point, followed her coffin to the grave with a few friends. On his return to the cottage he collapsed.

· · ·

Then he lapsed into a state of fever or of delirium. He told an admirer, six weeks later, "I was overwhelmed by a sorrow so poignant as to deprive me for several weeks of all power of thought or action." Maria Clemm wrote to

Mrs. Shew imploring her aid. "Eddie says you promised Virginia to come every other day for a long time," she said, "or until he was able to go to work again. I hope and believe you will not fail him."

Mrs. Shew was so alarmed by his condition that she expected him to succumb. She believed that he suffered from a "lesion" on his brain, which on occasions might provoke madness. She raised another subscription on his behalf, and helped to nurse him through his nervous prostration. She believed fish was a sovereign remedy for "brain fever," as it was known, but she also offered more spiritual consolations. She persuaded him to attend a midnight service with her, but on the recital of the words "he was a man of sorrows and acquainted with grief," Poe rushed out of the church. He was not, in any case, a man of conventional religious beliefs. He had never willingly attended a church service in his life. Maria Clemm claimed that she had "wished to die" in this period, but that she "*had* to live to take care of . . . poor disconsolate Eddie."

There was one small consolation. In a bizarre but unavoidable chain of events (which in other circumstances he might have relished), Poe's libel suit against the *Mirror* was heard before the New York Superior Court on the day before Virginia's funeral. In his deposition against Poe, Thomas Dunn English reported the character of Poe to be "that of a notorious liar, a common drunkard and of one utterly lost to all the obligations of honour." These were serious charges, enough to uproot any reputation Poe might have acquired in New York. But the jurors were not disposed to believe English. The case went in Poe's favour. One witness denied ever having said the words reported of him. Another testified that he had "never heard anything against him except that he is occasionally addicted to intoxication." But drunkenness did not imply either forgery or larceny. The jurors found for the plaintiff, and returned a verdict of $225.06 in libel damages and $101.42 in costs. It was one of the largest single sums of money that Poe had ever received. "Pretty well," he said, "considering that there was *no* actual 'damage' done to me." He went out and purchased a new suit—black, as always—as well as a carpet and table for the cottage in Fordham.

He was not out of danger, however. Mrs. Shew continued to visit him and to nurse him. According to her later account Poe would speak continually of the past. But it was not his true past. He told her that he had fought a duel over a woman in France. He told her that he had been rescued from subsequent illness by a cultured Scotswoman, who had visited him daily for thirteen weeks. He told her that he had written an autobiographical novel, *Life of an Unfortunate Artist*, that had been falsely credited to the pen of Eugene Sue. He told her, also, that his "beautiful mother" had been born at sea. He added that "it was the regret of his life, that he had not vindicated his mother to the world." This may or may not be an allusion to the supposed illegitimacy of his sister. But, in his excited state, it does not really matter. From his earliest life he harboured within himself an emptiness—a yearning for consolation and love and protection. And at the same time he was lost in the world, fantasising about his identity.

Slowly he recovered. Maria Clemm would sit beside him as he lay restless in his bed, continually smoothing his brow and applying "soothing" lotions to his forehead.

. . .

There are many reminiscences of his new life at Fordham, in the company of Maria Clemm and Catterina the cat. Catterina would settle herself on his shoulders, while he was writing, and purr with delight. A visitor said that "she seemed possessed." Poe entertained visitors with tea, and took rambles with them along the banks of the Bronx River. On one occasion he engaged in a game of leaping, at which he had excelled as a schoolboy; he excelled again, but at the cost of a pair of broken gaiters. He sat on a garden seat beneath the cherry tree, whistling to the pet birds whose cages hung in the branches. He ate fruit, and buttermilk, and curds. He told one correspondent that "I have never been so well . . . I rise early, eat moderately, drink nothing but water, and take abundant and regular exercise in the open air."

Now he needed to restore his life. One cause of drinking and of despair had at least been removed. In a letter he wrote some months after Virginia's funeral he revealed that he had been intoxicated even to madness and "I had indeed, nearly abandoned all hope of a permanent cure when I found one in the *death* of my wife." This might have been a line out of his fiction, but the truth was there. It was the crippling anxiety induced by her condition, and the fatal progress from hope to despair, that had materially influenced his drinking. Now, he said, "my ambition is great." Once more he began to revive hopes of publishing his own literary magazine.

In the summer of 1847 he visited Washington and Philadelphia with the intention both of gaining sub-scribers and of placing articles in the local magazines. He was spotted in the garden of the Episcopal High School in Virginia, near Washington, and was persuaded to recite "The Raven" to "the delight of all who were present." Without the restraining presence of Maria Clemm, how-ever, and despite his own earnest protestations, he fell back into drink. To one associate in Philadelphia he wrote, on returning to Fordham, "Without your aid, at the precise moment and in the precise manner in which you rendered it, it is more than probable that I should not now be alive to write you this letter . . ." He said that he was "exceed-ingly ill—so much so that I had no hope except in getting home immediately." "Ill" was often, for Poe, a euphemism for being drunk. No force on earth could now restrain him from the bottle. There was never any connection between his protestations and his behaviour, just as there was no re-lation between his reminiscences and his real life. His words sprang freely from his imagination, his actions from need and obscure desire.

During these months at Fordham, however, away from the temptations of the bottle, he began to contemplate a long scientific essay. On 3 February 1848, the newspapers of New York announced that Poe would be lecturing that evening on "The Universe" at the Society Library on the corner of Broadway and Leonard Street. The proceeds were supposed to help to finance the *Stylus*. But it was a stormy night, and only sixty people attended. Poe spoke for some two and a half hours on the mysteries of the cosmos, and one young lawyer in the audience recalled "his pale, delicate, intellectual face and magnificent eyes. His lecture was a rhapsody of the most intense brilliancy. He appeared inspired, and his inspiration affected the scant audience almost painfully. He wore his coat tightly buttoned across his slender chest . . ."

The newspaper accounts were on the whole laudatory, although it is not at all clear that the journalists present fully grasped Poe's analysis of "divine essence" and "infinite space." Yet the *Morning Express* concluded that "this brilliant effort was greeted with warm applause by the audience, who had listened with enchained attention throughout." Others were not so enthusiastic. One contemporary regarded it as "a mountainous piece of absurdity for a popular lecture." Of the newspaper reviews Poe commented that "all praised it . . . and all absurdly misrepresented it." He predicted that his work would be appreciated two thousand years hence. Nevertheless Poe was emboldened by its more immediate success. Two months later he approached George P. Putnam in his publishing offices on Broadway.

Putnam recalled the meeting when Poe "seated at my

desk, and looking at me a full minute with his 'glittering eye' he at length said 'I am Mr Poe.' I was 'all ear,' of course, and sincerely interested." Poe then paused. "I hardly know," he said, "how to begin what I have to say. It is a matter of profound importance." He then went on to claim that he proposed the publication of a work that would throw into the shade Newton's discovery of gravitation, and that the book "would at once command such universal and intense attention that the publisher might give up all other enterprises, and make this one book the business of his lifetime." He proposed a first printing of fifty thousand copies. Putnam was "impressed" but not "overcome," he said, and promised a response two days later. Then Poe asked him for a small loan.

Putnam thought over the matter, purchased the manuscript, and eventually printed five hundred copies of *Eureka*.

In the meantime Poe lingered in New York. He dined with his literary friend Rufus Griswold and unfortunately became inebriated. He sent a request for assistance to Mrs. Shew, who dispatched a doctor and a friend to minister to him. They "found him crazy-drunk in the hands of the police, and took him home to Fordham (eleven miles), where we found poor Mrs. Clemm waiting for him." He had been away from home for three days, and had spent all the money given to him. So his rescuers left Maria Clemm five dollars for immediate necessities.

Mrs. Shew was in any case reaching the limit of her toleration for the eccentricities of her erstwhile patient.

She never complained of his drunkenness or his excitability; for her these were merely the symptoms of a fatally weakened constitution. But she objected to Poe's beliefs, stated in his lecture on the universe. He had already prepared his notes for publication, and at the end of his discussion he made a clear argument for a version of pantheism. A clerical friend of Mrs. Shew, the Reverend John Henry Hopkins, had discussed the matter with Poe. In a letter to Mrs. Shew he described how "a strange thrill nerved and dilated for an instant his slight figure, as he exclaimed, 'My whole nature utterly *revolts* at the ideas that there is any Being in the Universe superior to *myself.*' " Poe was hardly a Christian at all.

This is not what the pious Mrs. Shew wished to hear. She could not consort with a heretic. Her trips to Fordham became infrequent. She became more formal, and more restrained. When she uttered a faint "amen" for the grace before dinner, Poe claimed that "I felt my heart stop, and I was sure I was then to die before your eyes." In the early summer Mrs. Shew sent him a letter of leavetaking. He replied that "for months I have known you were deserting me." It should be remembered that, of all the calamities he most feared, that of female withdrawal was by far the most painful. It was connected with the death of his mother, and the deaths of the other young women to whom he had been devoted. So to Mrs. Shew he called out as from the depths—"for me alas! Unless some true and tender and pure womanly love saves me, I shall hardly last a year longer!" He added that "it is too late you are floating away with the cruel tide. I am a coward to write this to you, but it is not a common trial, it is a fearful one to me." It was the last letter she ever received from him.

Even before Mrs. Shew's defection, however, Poe had been surveying the horizon for another and more impressionable young woman. In May 1848, he wrote an impassioned if not exactly passionate letter to Jane E. Locke; he called her "Sweet friend, dear friend" and alluded ruefully to his "hermit life . . . buried in the woods of Fordham." He claimed that "my whole existence has been the merest Romance—in the sense of the most utter unworldliness." He wanted to learn more, much more, about her personal history. There was one question "which I 'dare not even ask' of you." That question was, no doubt, concerning her marital status. It turned out that she was married. She went from being "My Dear Friend" to "My Dear Mrs. Locke." His plans had again been thwarted. But within a few weeks he was set to try again.

. . .

Eureka was published in the summer of 1848. It was the last of his works to be issued in his lifetime, and is in certain respects the most puzzling. The confusion is not helped by his preface in which he declared the composition to be "an Art-Product alone: let us say as a Romance; or, if I be not urging too lofty a claim, as a Poem." It purports to be an account of the origin and the history of the universe, couched in the most recondite prose, but it is also a record of the obsessions and preoccupations that had animated Poe's fiction and poetry. It begins with the general proposition that, *"In the Original Unity of the First Things lies the Secondary Cause of All Things, with the Germ of their Inevitable Annihilation."* Poe surveyed the universality of gravitation before suggesting that the gravitational principle was simply one manifestation of the desire of all things to return to some original state of unity. "I am not so sure that I speak and see," he wrote, "that my heart beats and my soul lives . . . as I am of the irretrievably bygone *Fact* that All Things and All Thoughts of Things, with all their ineffable Multiplicity of Relation, sprang at once into being from the primordial and irrelative *One*." But all things yearn to return to that original "unity" and that primaeval "nothingness" or, as he put it, "their source lies in the principle, *Unity. This* is their lost parent." The reference to "lost parent" may be significant. Was he contemplating that yearned-for return to the mother? There may be some buried allusion to his own loss in the belief that a "diffusion from Unity, under the conditions, involves a tendency to return into Unity—a tendency ineradicable until satisfied." Is there perhaps here some explanation for his excessive drinking, in the desire to return to some state of infantile bliss and tactility?

But then in the return to that original unity, that womb, "the processes we have here ventured to contemplate will be renewed forever, and forever, and forever; a novel Universe swelling into existence, and then subsiding into nothingness, at every throb of the Heart Divine. And now—this Heart Divine—what is it? *It is our own*." The tell-tale heart beats within Poe, and within every one of us. The universe is within us. It is an ancient doctrine, which Poe might have derived from Paracelsus or from Blake, but it is likely to have been found anew by Poe himself. In a letter to one correspondent he stated that "What I have propounded will (in good time) revolutionise the world of Physical and Metaphysical Science. I say this calmly—but I say it." Some cosmologists have claimed that Poe is the harbinger of Einstein and the first theorist of "black holes," but it might be suggested that Poe is simply applying his ever restless and perplexed imagination to the world of matter and of spirit. He added, in this context, "The plots of God are perfect. The Universe is a plot of God." Poe gives himself too little credit.

. . .

In the same period Poe composed two of his most famous poems, "Ulalume" and "The Bells," that come as close to "sound poetry" as any verse he ever wrote. It is said that he designed the first of them as an exercise in elocution or recitation, and that in the other he wished to reproduce the effect of the pealing of bells. He told some journalists in Richmond that he wished "to express in language the exact sounds of bells to the ears." In both cases he succeeded, but at the cost of sense and perhaps of significance. They are exercises in "pure poetry," where cadence and the suggestive melody of rhyme are employed for their own sake. He wished to create "this poem which is a poem and nothing more—this poem written solely for the poem's sake." Its object was pleasure, not truth, and its effect was one of indefinite rather than definite pleasure; it consisted solely in "the *Rhythmical Creation of Beauty*." This theory is equivalent to the doctrine of art for art's sake, adumbrated by Pater and Swinburne for a later generation. Yet there was something more. There was also his statement that "the origin of Poetry lies in a thirst for a wilder Beauty than Earth supplies," for a "supernal Loveliness" to be glimpsed in "the glories beyond the grave"; he is invoking the yearning for something irremediably lost, something missing for ever.

His late poems, then, could be seen as complementary to his speculations in *Eureka*. It was poetry like this that appealed to the French Symbolist poets and guaranteed his preeminent reputation among poets such as Baudelaire and Mallarmé. But the same work was less enthusiastically received by Anglo-American poets and critics, who have deemed it "juvenile" or a form of "nonsense poetry" in the line of Edward Lear. That disparity of judgement exists still.

CHAPTER TEN

The Women

The departure of Mrs. Shew, and the false start with Mrs. Locke, had not materially affected Poe's passionate desire for female companionship. In the summer of 1848 he visited Mrs. Locke and her husband at Lowell, in Massachusetts, where he was about to deliver a lecture on "The Poets and Poetry of America." Mrs. Locke then introduced him to a neighbour, a young woman named Annie Richmond. At a later date, in a fictional essay, he claimed that he was smitten at first sight. "As she approached, with a certain modest description of step almost indescribable, I said to myself, Surely here I have found the perfection of natural, in contradistinction from artificial *grace* . . . So intense an expression of *romance*, perhaps I should call it, or of unworldliness, as that which gleamed from her deep-set eyes, had never so sunk into my heart of hearts before." Her eyes were "spiritual." Perhaps he deemed her even capable of an early death.

After he had given his lecture he spent the rest of that evening, and much of the following day, with Annie Richmond. He may also have been in the company of her husband and her brother, but that does not seem to have lessened his enthusiasm. Jane Locke had already been forgotten. Annie Richmond herself recalled that "he seemed so unlike any other person . . . all the events of his life, which he narrated to me, had a flavour of *unreality* about them, just like his stories." They may have been much closer to his fiction than she ever imagined. He was permanently incomplete, passionately attaching himself to anyone who showed affection or even kindness. Hence his espousal of abstract "beauty" as the source of all wisdom and consolation. But at the same time he was a ferocious analyst and calculator of his position, examining all the objects that made up his prison.

In the same month as his meeting with Annie Richmond, for example, he made discreet enquiries about Sarah Helen Whitman, a poet from Providence, Rhode Island, who had lately sent him a Valentine poem. He asked one correspondent, "Can you not tell me something about her—anything—everything you know . . ." The tone of his letter suggests that he was in a state of some desperation: he needed the love and comfort of someone, anyone, with whom he felt a poetic affinity. He was the orphan crying for more.

Then in July he travelled down to Richmond, his boyhood home, ostensibly to gather subscribers for his literary magazine. There are reports of his drinking, however, and of his reciting passages from *Eureka* in the public bars and taverns. One contemporary, the editor of the *Southern Literary Messenger*, reported that "his entire residence in Richmond of late was but a succession of disgraceful follies." This sounds like an exaggeration.

He was collected enough, for example, to seek an interview with one of his erstwhile loves. Elmira Royster, by whom he had been enamoured before he had gone to the University of Virginia, had now become an affluent widow, Mrs. Shelton. She recalled later that Poe was excited by their meeting after many years. "He came up to me in the most enthusiastic manner and said, 'Oh!, Elmira, is this you.'" It is likely that he considered proposing to her, but a newly composed poem from the other widow, Sarah Helen Whitman, changed his plans. It concluded with the immortal line, "I dwell with '*Beauty which is Hope.*'" After he received the poem, through the agency of Maria Clemm, he left Richmond and made his way towards Providence. We may apply to him what he wrote to an earlier correspondent: "You need not attempt to shake off, or to banter off, Romance. It is an evil you will never get rid of to the end of your days. It is a part of your self—a portion of your soul." And so it proved for Poe.

Mrs. Whitman possessed an ethereal temper. She was known as the "Seeress of Providence"—whether the town, or futurity itself, is open to question. She was distracted and absentminded; she swathed herself in veils, which invariably became entangled, and was continually dropping or losing little items such as fans and shawls. She was said to flutter "like a bird." She was a great exponent of table rapping and other communications beyond the grave. She was also addicted to ether, with which she liberally soaked her handkerchiefs in more than usually distressing moments. There were many such moments ready to engulf her.

Poe reached New York at the beginning of September 1848, and wished to satisfy himself that Helen Whitman was in residence at Providence by sending an anonymous letter asking for her autograph. It was one of the little "hoaxes" that he enjoyed. Two weeks later he presented himself in person, with a formal letter of introduction from a mutual friend. Then he gave her a signed volume of *The Raven and Other Poems* with a dedication "from the most devoted of her friends. Edgar A. Poe." The next morning they visited the Athenaeum Library where Mrs. Whitman, somewhat disingenuously, asked him whether he had ever read "Ulalume." To her infinite surprise, Poe revealed himself to be the author.

That evening Poe was introduced to the circle of Helen Whitman's closest friends. One of those present recalled that "Poe and Helen were greatly agitated. Simultaneously both arose from their chairs and walked towards the center of the room. Meeting, he held her in his arms, kissed her; they stood for a moment, then he led her to her seat. There was a dead silence through all this strange proceeding."

On the following day they visited a local cemetery, overlooking the Seekonk River. In these affecting sur-

roundings Poe proposed marriage. Helen Whitman recalled later that "he endeavoured . . . to persuade me that
my influence and my presence would have power to lift his
life out of the torpor of despair which had weighed upon
him, and give an inspiration to his genius, of which he had
as yet given no token." She declined, or perhaps prevaricated, citing the need to support an elderly mother. She
promised instead to write to him, with a fuller explanation.
Two days later Poe left for New York, to which place he
was followed by a letter from Mrs. Whitman claiming that
she was too old and too fragile to become the second Mrs.
Poe. She was in fact only six years his senior, but the
protestation of a weak nervous constitution rings true. He
was not a man for a faint-hearted female.

On the following day Poe replied in a letter of several
thousand words, beginning "I have pressed your letter
again and again to my lips, sweetest. Helen—bathing it in
tears of joy or of a 'divine despair.' " There was a great
deal more in the same vein of theatrical, or elevated, sen-
timent in the course of which he renewed his claim for her
affections and insisted that under his care she "would get
better, and finally well." He also provided her with a pot-
ted history of their brief relationship, recounting his emotions on first seeing her in Providence where "I felt, for
the first time in my life, and tremblingly acknowledged, the
existence of spiritual influences altogether out of the
reach of reason. I saw that you were *Helen—my* Helen—
the Helen of a thousand dreams."

Helen Whitman replied eight days later, once more excusing herself from marriage on the grounds that she had taken responsibility for her mother and her unmarried younger sister. She could not abandon them for married life, however high-minded. She also asked Poe, somewhat tactlessly, the reason for his bad reputation among certain people. She had heard it said that "he has great intellectual power, but *no* principle—*no* moral sense."

He replied at once, with another extraordinarily long and impassioned letter. He interpreted the eight days' delay as a token of the fact that *"You do not love me."* He lamented "that my heart is broken—that I have no farther object in life—that I have absolutely no wish but to die." He was particularly upset about Mrs. Whitman's questions concerning his moral character. "Until the moment when these horrible words first met my eye," he claimed, "I would not have believed it possible that any such opinions could have existed at all . . ." Since he had regularly viewed similar opinions in the public prints, and had even instigated a suit for libel, his surprise was a little forced.

He promised to reveal "the truth or nothing." He claimed that "I deliberately threw away from me a large fortune, rather than endure a trivial wrong." Of his marriage to Virginia Clemm he stated that "I did violence to my own heart, and married for another's happiness, when I knew that no possibility of my own existed." There was very little "truth" in either statement, and the second complaint reads like a monstrous betrayal of his first wife. There then followed some obscure hints about his relationship with Fanny Osgood. It was by his standards a poor performance. It is certain that for him words, and the cadence of words, created their own reality. In the process of composition he may have believed it all. But here he was rewriting and revising his own life.

In "Berenice" the narrator confesses that "my passions always were of the mind," and we may infer this to be a partial diagnosis of Poe's own condition. His yearnings were always of an idealised and spiritual nature. In his work, he was never interested in any sensual pleasure. In his life, whenever any physical union seemed to become a possibility, he fled into drink. A contemporary described him as "of all the men that I ever knew, he was the most *passionless*." In his art and in his life, he fell in love with dying women.

Even before Helen Whitman received the letter, Poe appeared before her. Once more he asked her to entertain his offer of marriage. He was on his way to Lowell, where he was about to deliver a lecture, and he asked her to send a further message to him there.

But, at Lowell itself, he was once more in the presence of the other woman whom he adored in equal measure—Annie Richmond. After spending a little time with Mr. and Mrs. Locke, he moved to Annie's house nearby. This change in his affections altogether disrupted his friendship with Jane Locke, but sealed that with Annie Richmond. He became her inseparable companion, and her sister recalled him "sitting before an open wood fire, in the early autumn evening, gazing intently into the glowing coal, holding the hand of a dear friend—'Annie'—while for a long time no one spoke." This may have been in the presence of Annie's compliant husband, who clearly deemed Poe to be no threat.

But Poe had also recently written to Helen Whitman that he would joyfully "go down *with* you into the night of the Grave."

A few days after his visit to Lowell he wrote a letter to Annie Richmond in which he asked, "Why am I not *with* you now *darling . . .*" His affections were infinitely malleable. He even consulted Annie Richmond on his future with Helen Whitman, and it seems that Mrs. Richmond counselled matrimony. He was not necessarily grateful, however, for her advice. "*Can* you, *my* Annie," he wrote, "bear to think I am another's?" He left her in "an agony of grief," and travelled once more to Providence.

Even before seeing Helen Whitman, he broke down. He endured a "long, long, hideous night of despair" before purchasing two ounces of laudanum the following morning. He travelled on to Boston, where he wrote a letter to Annie in which he reminded her of her "promise that under all circumstances, you would come to me on my bed of death." So he implored her to come at once to Boston, and named the place where he could be found. He seemed seriously to be contemplating suicide. But he was principally reacting to the thought of actually going through with the marriage to Helen Whitman. He explained to Annie "how my soul revolted from saying the words which were to be said." Then he swallowed an ounce of the laudanum.

The effects were immediate and profound, suggesting that contrary to rumour he was not an inveterate taker of opium. His cousin, Elizabeth Herring, indicated that during the period of Virginia's illness he was "often in sad condition from the use of opium." It was a natural reaction to his anxiety and despair. It would in fact be surprising if he had not used opium or tincture of laudanum occasionally, given its efficacy and ready availability. It would have been a useful alternative to alcohol. But the evidence does not suggest that he was an habitual imbiber of the drug. On this occasion in Boston, for example, he lost command of his reason and an unnamed "friend" helped him to cope with "the awful horrors which succeeded."

Two days later, on 7 November, he was composed enough to journey to Providence. Helen Whitman was too agitated to see him, having been troubled by his absence of two days. So he sent her a note ordering her to "write me *one word* to say that you *do* love me and that, *under all circumstances*, you will be mine." The changes in his mood are bewildering and extreme; they do suggest, at the very least, a temporary derangement fuelled either by the laudanum or by alcohol. She agreed to meet him, at the Athenaeum library, half an hour later. In the course of this interview he recounted all that had happened to him in Boston. They met again in the afternoon, when Mrs. Whitman once more prevaricated over his proposal of marriage. She also read him a letter, from someone in New York, in which his character had been abused. He seemed "deeply pained."

That evening Poe began drinking. In his intoxicated

state he despatched a "note of renunciation and farewell" to Mrs. Whitman. She assumed that he had travelled back to New York, but he had in fact stayed at Providence in the care of a Mr. MacFarlane. MacFarlane, on the following morning, persuaded Poe to sit for a daguerreotype. It shows him quizzical, sarcastic, subdued with that strange alteration in both halves of his visage. His face looks puffy, there are rings under his eyes, his mouth seems twisted in a sneer, his eyes are deep-set and thoughtful. After being photographed Poe rushed around to Helen Whitman's house "in a state of wild & delirious excitement, calling upon me to save him from some terrible impending doom." His voice was "appalling . . . never have I heard anything so awful, even to sublimity." He was in the throes of a condition akin to madness.

Mrs. Whitman's mother sat with him for two hours, in an attempt to calm him, but when Helen eventually entered the room "he clung to me so frantically as to tear away a piece of the muslin dress I wore." A doctor was called, and he diagnosed "cerebral congestion." Poe was then removed to the house of a friend of Mrs. Whitman, where he recuperated for two or three days. There were several more interviews, during which Helen agreed to a "conditional engagement"—the condition being that Poe stopped drinking altogether. But Helen's mother was stubbornly opposed to the match, telling Poe that her daughter's death would be preferable to any union with him. On the evening of 13 November, frustrated in his muddled desire for marriage, Poe left on a steamer for New York.

From New York he composed a note to Mrs. Whitman, explaining that he felt "your dear love at my heart" but that he sensed "a strange shadow of coming evil." He then took the train to Fordham, where he was at last reunited with Maria Clemm. Mrs. Clemm wrote to Annie Richmond saying that "God has . . . returned my poor darling Eddy to me. But how changed! I scarcely knew him." Poe also wrote to Annie another long and agonised letter, in which he said that "you *know* I love you, as no man ever loved woman . . . oh, *my darling, my* Annie, my own sweet *sister* Annie, my *pure* beautiful angel—*wife* of my soul . . ."

But he had not entirely lost his sense of reality. Four days later he was writing to a putative benefactor, asking for two hundred dollars for the establishment of his proposed literary magazine. He slowly began to recover from the excitement induced by recent events, his composure only slightly ruffled by the news that Helen Whitman's mother had taken entire control of the Whitman estate.

. . .

Then on 20 December, Poe returned to Providence in order to deliver a lecture on "The Poetic Principle." Any other motive must remain in doubt. One poet of his acquaintance, Mary E. Hewitt, asked if he was also going to Providence for his marriage. He is supposed to have replied, "That marriage will never take place." He lectured before some eighteen hundred people in the Franklin Lyceum, with Mrs. Whitman among the audience. On the following day she agreed to an "immediate marriage," with the familiar stipulation that he would never drink again. Poe attended an evening reception at her home, where he remained very quiet. On the morning of the next day he was seen to take a glass of wine. He called upon Helen, with profuse apologies. The apologies were apparently accepted, for on the following day he wrote a note to the minister of the local Episcopal church asking him to publish the banns for the forthcoming marriage. Poe then wrote to Maria Clemm that "we shall be married on Monday [Christmas Day], and will be at Fordham on Tuesday."

These well-laid plans came to nothing. On the day he had written to Maria Clemm, he had ridden out in a carriage with his intended bride. They visited one of the many libraries in the city, where a note was placed in Mrs. Whitman's hand. It was a "poison pen" letter of the most vicious kind, informing her "of many things in Mr. Poe's recent career" and in particular of his continued drinking. It may also have alluded to his association with Annie Richmond. This was too great a strain for Helen Whitman. When they returned to the Whitman home, she stupefied herself with ether and sank upon the sofa. Poe knelt down beside her, and begged for one word.

"What *can* I say?"

"Say that you love me, Helen."

"*I love you.*"

Then the unhappy and confused woman collapsed into unconsciousness.

Poe had a less passionate interview with Mrs. Whitman's mother, in which she made it very clear that his presence was no longer required. The result was that he left the house, complaining of "intolerable insults," and boarded the steamer to New York. He never saw Helen Whitman again.

It is a strange story, rendered even more bizarre by Poe's baffling and incoherent conduct. He was writing passionate and devoted letters to two women at the same time, promising undying love to both. He was like a cuttlefish floundering in its own ink. He had traduced his dead wife's memory. He had expressed the wish to die in Annie Richmond's arms; he had expressed something like infantile dependence upon both women. And, significantly, he knew well enough that both women were ultimately unobtainable. In that respect, at least, they resembled the idealised image of his own mother. There was one difference. To Helen, in his signatures, he was "Edgar." To Annie, he was "Eddy." It is as if two people inhabited the same body—the adult Edgar and the infant Eddy. It was Eddy who wrote that "I need not tell you, Annie, how great a burden is taken off my heart by my rupture with Mrs. W . . ."

There was one further complication. The family of Annie Richmond's husband lived in Providence, and were busily retelling all the gossip about Poe and Helen Whitman, including the information that Mrs. Whitman had withdrawn the marriage banns. This was untrue. The marriage banns had never been published at all. But the suspicion was, of course, that it was Mrs. Whitman, not Poe, who had sundered their relationship and that she had done so on the basis of some new evidence against him. Poe wrote to Helen Whitman towards the end of January 1849, explaining "that *you* Mrs. W have uttered, promulgated or in any way countenanced this pitiable falsehood, I do not & cannot believe . . . It has been my intention to say simply, that our marriage was postponed on account of your ill health."

Perhaps on the same day Poe wrote to Annie Richmond complaining that "I felt *deeply* wounded by the cruel statements of your letter." He enclosed his letter to Mrs. Whitman, which he had post-dated, asking Annie to read it, seal it, and send it on. It was his best opportunity of clearing his name. Helen Whitman never replied.

CHAPTER ELEVEN

The Last Year

He was trying to look ahead. In February 1849 he wrote a relatively optimistic letter to his old friend Frederick Thomas, in which he claimed that "I shall be a *litterateur* at least all my life." In the same period he told Annie Richmond that "I have not suffered a day to pass without writing from a page to three pages." By the spring he completed the final version of "The Bells" and began the poem he entitled "Annabel Lee"; he was also writing one of his most peculiar stories, "Hop Frog," about the vengeance wreaked by a dwarfish clown forced to entertain various noble and royal patrons. He also wrote a "hoaxing" story, "Von Kempelen and His Discovery," on the possibility of turning lead into gold. He claimed that he had not been drinking and, indeed, that he was "in better health than I ever knew myself to be." He and Maria Clemm had taken the cottage at Fordham for another year. There was another reason for confidence. A prospective patron for the *Stylus* had unexpectedly emerged. A young admirer of Poe, Edward Patterson of Oquawka, Illinois, had offered to subsidise a literary magazine under Poe's exclusive control. Poe wrote back in enthusiastic terms. All would be well.

But then there came the inevitable reaction. The journals, from which he had been hoping for funds for his contributions, collapsed one after the other. By April Poe had become once more seriously unwell. "I thought," Maria Clemm wrote to Annie Richmond, "he would *die* several times." He had relapsed into nervous despair. He reported to Annie that "my sadness is *unaccountable,* and this makes me the more sad. *Nothing* cheers or comforts me. My life seems wasted—the future looks a dreary blank." It was the necessary response to that period of hysterical turmoil in his twin pursuit of Annie Richmond and Helen Whitman.

Yet once more he travelled down to Richmond, in order to deliver a series of lectures. He may also have welcomed the opportunity of renewing his approaches to Elmira Shelton, the wealthy widow who had once been his belle. And he wanted to find new subscribers for the proposed journal. "I am now going to Richmond," he told one correspondent, "to 'see about it.'"

So, on 29 June 1849, Maria Clemm saw him off on the steamboat to Philadelphia. His words of farewell, according to her memory, were "God bless my own darling Muddy do not fear for your Eddy see how good I will be while I am away from you, and will come back to love and comfort you." He was, essentially, going home. She never saw him again.

. . .

He had intended to travel through Philadelphia on his way to Richmond, but a recurrence of his old sickness detained him. He began to drink. His suitcase, which contained two of the lectures he was about to deliver at Richmond, was lost at the railway station. This was not a good sign. The next two or three days are enveloped in a haze. Poe told Maria Clemm, in an hysterical letter written a week later from Philadelphia, that "I have been taken to prison once since I came here for getting drunk; but *then* I was not. It was about Virginia." The only problem with his confession is that the available prison records show no evidence of Poe ever being arrested. In turn it has been suggested that he was detained for his own safety; that he was recognised in court, and acquitted. But the most likely explanation seems to be that Poe was suffering from delirium tremens or some form of paranoiac hallucination.

On the day after his supposed arrest, for example, he called upon an old acquaintance, the engraver and publisher John Sartain, looking "pale and haggard, with a wild and frightened expression in his eyes." He pleaded with him for protection and explained that "some men" were about to assassinate him. Then in his tormented state he entertained the prospect of suicide and asked Sartain for a razor. He wished only to shave off his moustache, however, so that he could escape detection from the possible murderers. Sartain then performed the deed with a pair of scissors. (Here we may entertain a cavil of doubt about Sartain's memory. Poe had a moustache on his arrival in Richmond soon afterwards.)

That evening they made an expedition to the local waterworks by the Schuylkill River where, according to Sartain's account, foolishly they mounted the steps to the reservoir. Poe then confided to him his visions, or hallucinations, while incarcerated in the Philadelphia jail. They included the sight of Maria Clemm being frightfully mutilated. He went into a "sort of convulsion," and Sartain had to help him carefully down the steep steps to safety.

Poe stayed with his protector for two or three nights, and on the second morning he was recovered sufficiently to leave the house unaccompanied. On his return he confided that his recent delusions were "created by his own excited imagination." Sartain may have already come to that conclusion. A few days later Poe wrote to Maria Clemm, complaining that "I have been so ill—have had the cholera, or spasms quite as bad." He asked her to come to him immediately on receipt of the letter, with the ominous warning that "we can but die together. It is no use to reason with me *now*; I must die." He sent the letter to the care of Sarah Anne Lewis, in Brooklyn, but Mrs. Lewis wisely did not pass it on to Maria Clemm. Mrs. Clemm, meanwhile, fretted and worried about poor Eddy.

Poe was still ill and impoverished. He visited a Philadelphia reporter, George Lippard, in his offices. He was wearing only one shoe. He had no money, and had not eaten. He said that he had no friends, having conveniently forgotten about Sartain. Lippard quickly raised some money from sympathetic local publishers, and Poe finally scraped together the fare to make his way to Richmond.

He found his suitcase at the railway station; but, to his dismay, it had been opened and his lectures stolen. It is not clear what thief would have been interested in Poe's lucubrations on the state of American poetry.

Richmond had been his destination all along, but he arrived much later than he expected. The whole experience in Philadelphia became for him a phantasmagoria of suffering, brought on by what he described as *"mania-a-potu,"* or alcoholic madness. It is the first indication that he realised the nature of his true condition. The sequence of events in Philadelphia is not at all clear, and it is not wise to take the later recollections of Sartain or of Lippard at face value. There is always much myth-making in stories of Poe. That he did face some kind of crisis, however, is not in doubt. Lippard later recalled that, on their leave-taking at Philadelphia, "there was in his voice, look and manner something of a Presentment that his strange and stormy life was near its close." This is known as the benefit of hindsight.

. . .

As soon as Poe arrived in Richmond he wrote to Maria Clemm, explaining that for the last weeks "your poor Eddy has scarcely drawn a breath except of intense agony." He added towards the end that "my clothes are *so horrible*, and I am so *ill*." Then five days later, he seems to have recovered his spirits. He was in better health and wrote to Maria Clemm that "all may yet go well. I will put forth all my energies." He had the most extraordinary powers of recuperation—or it may be that the wild alterations in his moods (and in his physical well-being) had more to do with words than with realities. He took lodgings in the Swan Tavern, and paid calls upon old friends and acquaintances. He renewed his ties with his sister, Rosalie, with whom he had previously lost contact. And he began earning money by lecturing. He was, in fact, something of a public figure. "Mr. Poe is a native of this city and was reared in our midst," one newspaper reported, ". . . he reappears among us with increased reputation, and a strong claim upon public attention." He reported to Maria Clemm, in August, that "I *never* was received with so much enthusiasm."

There are several descriptions of him in Richmond, generally of a contrary quality. To one contemporary he seemed "invariably cheerful, and frequently playful in mood." To another his mouth displayed "firmness mingled with an element of scorn and discontent." In general he was, when sober, cordial and courteous; he seemed rarely to smile, but to exercise an overwhelming self-control. There was "much sadness in the intonation of the voice." There were times when he lapsed into old habits. On one occasion he was taken so ill from excessive consumption of alcohol that he had to be nursed by friends. It was said by a Richmond contemporary that for some days "his life was in imminent danger" and that it was the opinion of his doctors that "another such attack would prove fatall." He is supposed to have replied that "if people would not tempt him, he would not fall." Under the circumstances, it was not perhaps the most convincing response. He spent some time in the offices of the *Richmond Examiner*, however, where he was surrounded by convivial spirits who might indeed have "tempted" him. Mint julep was a favourite drink in Richmond.

He was sturdy enough, however, to renew his advances towards Elmira Shelton. He called upon her several times, and by the summer there were widespread rumours that he had become engaged to her. One contemporary reported, at a later date, that "the lady was a widow, of wealth and beauty, who was an old flame of his." But the path of true love is not often smooth. Two of Mrs. Shelton's children apparently opposed the match, and her dead husband had bequeathed his estate to her on condition that she did not remarry. Poe's intentions were also not entirely clear. He wrote a letter to Maria Clemm in which he suggested that she leave Fordham and remove herself to Richmond. And he added that "I want to live near Annie . . . Do not tell me anything about Annie—I cannot bear to hear it now—unless you can tell me that Mr. R. is dead." So on the brink of an engagement with Elmira Shelton he was still expressing his devotion to another woman. Three weeks later he had softened somewhat towards Mrs. Shelton. "I think she loves me more devotedly than any one I ever knew," he wrote to Maria

Clemm, "& I cannot help loving her in return. Nothing is yet definitely settled." Four days later, on 22 September, an engagement was tentatively envisaged. On the same day Elmira Shelton wrote to Maria Clemm explaining that "I am fully prepared to *love* you, and I do sincerely hope that our spirits may be congenial." She assured her that Poe was "sober, temperate, moral, & much beloved." So he had made a considerable effort to reassure his new inamorata. On the same day, too, it was reported that he had joined the local temperance society.

He was invited to lecture on "The Poetic Principle," two days later, and Mrs. Shelton sat in the front row before his lectern. A contemporary noted "her straight features, high forehead and cold expression of countenance . . . a sensible, practical woman, the reverse of a poet's ideal." And so it proved. Mrs. Shelton said later, when questioned about the alleged affair, that "I was not engaged to Poe when he left here, but there was a partial understanding, but I do not think I should have married him under any circumstances." As in all matters concerning Poe, the stories are convoluted and difficult to unravel.

. . .

There was another task to which he had to attend. A piano manufacturer from Philadelphia, John Loud, had offered Poe one hundred dollars for the task of editing a volume of his wife's poems. As Poe had written to Maria Clemm at the time, "Of course, I accepted his offer." So he was planning to leave Richmond for a while, to complete this remunerative but no doubt wearisome task. He calculated that it would take him three days. He also wished to travel on to New York, where he would make preparations for his new literary magazine.

Two evenings before he left Richmond he visited some old friends, the Talleys, to whom he expressed himself confident and hopeful. He declared that "the last few weeks in the society of his old and new friends had been the happiest that he had known for many years" and that he believed he was about to "leave behind all the trouble and vexation of his past life." Susan Talley had a postscript to this cheerful meeting. "He was the last of the party to leave the house. We were standing on the portico, and after going a few steps he paused, turned, and again lifted his hat, in a last adieu. At the moment, a brilliant meteor appeared in the sky directly over his head, and vanished in the east."

On the following evening, the last before his departure, he visited Elmira Shelton. At a later date she wrote to Maria Clemm explaining that "he was very sad, and complained of being quite sick. I felt his pulse, and found he had considerable fever." Mrs. Shelton believed that he was too ill to travel the next day but, to her chagrin and surprise, she discovered that he had indeed taken the steamboat to Baltimore. He was beginning the fateful journey that would end in his death, as related in the first chapter of this book. He was found, six days later, slumped in a tavern in Baltimore. No one knew where he had been, or what he had done. Had he been wandering, dazed, through the city? Had he been enlisted for the purposes of vote-rigging in a city notorious for its political chicanery? Had he suffered from a tumour of the brain? Had he simply drunk himself into oblivion? It is as tormenting a mystery as any to be found in his tales. He died in a hospital, on Sunday, 7 October 1849, a sad and beleaguered end to an unhappy and harassed life. He was forty years old.

. . .

On the day after his burial Maria Clemm wrote to Mrs. Richmond, "ANNIE, my Eddy *is dead*. He died in Baltimore yesterday. Annie! Pray for me, your desolate friend. My senses *will leave me*."

She may have been following Poe's stated wishes when she left the work of collecting Poe's papers to Rufus Griswold, but the decision had profound consequences for Poe's posthumous reputation. Griswold composed a memoir, as a preface to the third volume of Poe's works, which was part slander and part abuse. The tone had been set in Griswold's obituary of Poe, published the day after the funeral, in which he stated that his death "will startle many, but *few will be grieved by it . . . he had few or no friends*." The vituperation of the memoir itself was such that it provoked several rejoinders, but the libels against Poe's name became common currency for the rest of the nineteenth century.

Charles Baudelaire once remarked that "this death was almost a suicide, a suicide prepared for a long time." In truth Poe believed himself to have been marked out by an unlucky destiny from the day of his birth. He had been well versed, from his early days, in what he once called "the iron clasped volume of Despair." In one of his earliest stories, "MS Found in a Bottle," his narrator had written that "it is evident that we are hurrying onward to some exciting knowledge—some never to be imparted secret, whose attainment is destruction." Poe was fated to die in ignominy. He was fated to die raving. He once said that "I have often thought I could distinctly hear the sound of the darkness as it stole over the horizon." That darkness was always rushing towards him.

Maria Clemm settled with the Richmonds for some time, and then became a guest in other sympathetic households; it is clear, however, that she sometimes wore out her welcome. Eventually she found a last refuge in the "Church Home and Infirmary" at Baltimore.

Poe's reputation continued to grow in the years immediately after his death, especially in England and in France. He profoundly affected Verlaine and Rimbaud; Mallarmé and Baudelaire both translated "The Raven" in homage to an American poet who in certain respects seemed to be a precursor of European Romanticism and in particular the harbinger of Symbolism and of Surrealism. Baudelaire declared that, on reading Poe's poems and stories, he had found "not simply certain subjects, which I had dreamed of, but *sentences* which I had thought out, written by him twenty years before." Rémy de Gourmont declared, in fact, that Poe belonged to French rather than to American literature. Valéry told Gide that "Poe is the only impeccable writer. He is never mistaken."

Tennyson described him as "the most original genius that America has produced," worthy to stand beside Catullus and Heine. Thomas Hardy considered him to be "the first to realise in full the possibility of the English language," and Yeats believed that he was "certainly the greatest of American poets." The science fiction works of Jules Verne and H.G. Wells are heavily indebted to him, and Arthur Conan Doyle paid tribute to Poe's mastery of the detective genre. Nietzsche and Kafka both honoured him, and glimpsed in his sad career the outline of their own suffering souls. He was admired by Fyodor Dostoyevsky, Joseph Conrad, and James Joyce, who saw in him the seeds of modern literature. The orphan, in the end, found his true family.

POE'S PRINCIPAL PUBLICATIONS

1827—Poe's first book, *Tamerlane and Other Poems*

1829—Poe's second book, *Al Aaraaf, Tamerlane and Minor Poems*

1831—Poe's *Poems*

1838 (July)—Poe's *The Narrative of Arthur Gordon Pym*

1839—Poe's *Tales of the Grotesque and Arabesque*

1843 (July)—Poe's *Prose Romances*

1845—Poe's *Tales* and *The Raven and Other Poems*

1848 (about 15 July)—Poe's prose poem, *Eureka*

BIBLIOGRAPHY

Hervey Allen: *Israfel. The Life and Times of Edgar Allan Poe.* Two volumes (London, 1927).

Harold Bloom (editor): *Edgar Allan Poe, Modern Critical Views* (New York, 1985).

Marie Bonaparte: *The Life and Works of Edgar Allan Poe* (London, 1985).

David Halliburton: *Edgar Allan Poe, A Phenomenological View* (Princeton, 1973).

Kevin J. Hayes (editor): *The Cambridge Companion to Edgar Allan Poe* (Cambridge, 2002).

Daniel Hoffman: *Poe, Poe, Poe, Poe, Poe, Poe* (New York, 1972).

Jeffrey Meyers: *Edgar Allan Poe* (London, 1992).

Sidney P. Moss: *Poe's Literary Battles* (Carbondale, Illinois, 1969).

John Ward Ostrom (editor): *The Letters of Edgar Allan Poe.* Two volumes (New York, 1966).

Mary E. Phillips: *Edgar Allan Poe the Man.* Two volumes (Chicago, 1926).

Una Pope-Hennessy: *Edgar Allan Poe* (London, 1934).

Arthur Hobson Quinn: *Edgar Allan Poe* (New York, 1941).

Kenneth Silverman: *Edgar A. Poe* (London, 1992).

Floyd Stovall: *Edgar Poe, the Poet* (Charlottesville, Virginia, 1969).

Julian Symons: *The Tell-Tale Heart* (London, 1978).

Dwight Thomas and David K. Jackson: *The Poe Log* (Boston, 1987).

Edward Wagenknecht: *Edgar Allan Poe, the Man Behind the Legend* (New York, 1963).

I.M. Walker (editor): *Edgar Allan Poe, The Critical Heritage* (London, 1986).

Unless otherwise stated, all works are by Poe.

A NOTE ABOUT THE AUTHOR

Peter Ackroyd is the biographer of William Shakespeare, T. S. Eliot, Dickens, Blake, and Thomas More, and the author of the bestselling *London: the Biography*. The subject of his previous *Brief Life* was Isaac Newton. He has won the Whitbread Biography Award, the Royal Society of Literature's William Heinemann Award (jointly), and the James Tait Black Memorial Prize, and is the holder of a CBE for services to literature. He is the author of *Thames: The Biography*. His novels include *The Last Testament of Oscar Wilde* (winner of the Somerset Maugham Award), *Hawksmoor* (Guardian Fiction Prize), *Chatterton* (short-listed for the Booker Prize), and most recently *The Fall of Troy*. He lives in London.

A NOTE ABOUT THE TYPE

This book has been typeset in Monotype Garamond, a version of the original Garamond first introduced in 1541. This beautiful, classic font has been a standard among book designers and printers for more than four hundred years. While opinion varies as to the role that typecutter Claude Garamond played in the development of the typeface that bears his name, there is no doubt that this font had great influence on other typeface evolution from the sixteenth century to the present.